The American Exploration and Travel Series

[*For a complete list, see page 112.*]

Journey Through the Rocky Mountains
and the Humboldt Mountains to the Pacific Ocean

# JOURNEY THROUGH THE ROCKY MOUNTAINS AND THE HUMBOLDT MOUNTAINS TO THE PACIFIC OCEAN

by Jacob H. Schiel

*Translated from the German
and Edited by Thomas N. Bonner*

NORMAN: UNIVERSITY OF OKLAHOMA PRESS

By Thomas N. Bonner

*Medicine in Chicago* (Madison, 1957)

(editor) *Journey Through the Rocky Mountains
and the Humboldt Mountains to the Pacific Ocean*
(Norman, 1959)

Library of Congress Catalog Card Number: 59–7490

Copyright 1959 by the University of Oklahoma Press,
Publishing Division of the University.
Composed and printed at Norman, Oklahoma, U.S.A.,
by the University of Oklahoma Press.
First edition.

FOR *Phillip Lynn Bonner*

*Editor's Introduction*

THE INTEREST of the European in exploration and adventure in that constantly shifting area known as the American Frontier has never been adequately told. To the cultivated European, the United States, at least to the Civil War, was a place of incredible novelty and fascination where a civilization in the making could be seen, observed, and described for the benefit of those unfortunate enough to stay behind. The gallery of pre-Civil War visitors included not only such distinguished figures as De Tocqueville, Trollope, Martineau, and Dickens but a great host of lesser men and women who went to the border of civilization to see for themselves what was happening in the Great Experiment across the ocean. These visitors were drawn from all walks of life and someday the story of the travels of European merchants, scientists, and professional men will be told to supplement the better-known accounts by European political and literary lights.

This book records the impressions of one forgotten German scientist who made a lengthy visit to America in the 1850's. Jacob Heinrich Schiel was born in 1813 in Stromberg, a pretty wine town in western Germany, then part of the Rhenish provinces of Prussia. He took a scientific degree at the University of Heidelberg, where at that time he might have encountered the first Americans to taste the heady wine of German scholarship. In 1845 he became a *Docent* at the same university, lecturing in chemistry and geology. At the end of the 1840's, the date is uncertain, he came to the United States and remained a full decade in this country, not returning to his teaching duties at Heidelberg until 1859. After further years of teaching at Heidelberg he settled finally in Baden-Baden, that picturesque spa and tourist center in the Black Forest, where he lived out the remainder of his life.[1] Records concerning his life and work are very scarce, despite the fact that he was the author of four books ranging from a textbook in organic chemistry to a study of the inductive logic of John Stuart Mill and numerous articles on chemical and geological subjects.

He published in 1859 the account of his journey through the Rocky Mountains and the Humboldt Range to the Pacific.[2] This is the story of his experiences as official geologist and surgeon for the Gunnison expedition, one of the several government exploration parties sent west in 1853 and 1854 to investigate possible Pacific railroad routes. Schiel was not the only German man of science to participate in these surveys. The artist-topographer F. W. Egloffstein participated in both the unofficial Frémont expedition of 1853 and the Beckwith exploration of the 41st parallel to California in 1854;[3] F. Creutzfeldt, a botanist, was a colleague of Schiel's

---

[1] Most of this information is taken from Johann Christian Poggendorff, *Biographisch-literarisches Handwörterbuch zur Geschichte der exakten Wissenschaften*, III, 1187.

[2] *Reise durch die Felsengebirge und die Humboldtgebirge nach dem Stillen Ocean* (Schaffhausen, Brodtmann'schen Buchhandlung, 1859).

[3] Edward S. Wallace, *The Great Reconnaissance*, 135. Wallace's account comes closest to exploring satisfactorily the role of artists and scientists on the frontier just before the Civil War.

on the Gunnison expedition until murdered with his captain in Utah; and Heinrich B. Möllhausen won a reputation as "the German Fenimore Cooper" for the literary and artistic talents he revealed in his reports and books based on the Whipple and other expeditions.[4]

It was not unusual in this period that a physician might act as naturalist or geologist for a government exploration since science was as yet quite unspecialized in America,[5] but it does seem curious in Schiel's case that a geologist should pass himself off as a surgeon. Schiel possessed no medical degree and practiced no medicine in Germany, although he was apparently quite familiar with diseases and their remedies, as this book reveals. In the geological report written by Schiel for inclusion in the official report of the expedition, his name is followed by "M.D." which could mean that Schiel had deceived his superiors as to his training or, more likely, his doctor's degree in philosophy was automatically taken for a medical degree by Americans unfamiliar with the German university system.

*Journey Through the Rocky Mountains* is of special interest for the reason that it is an early book about the transMississippi West written by a German for a German audience. The descriptions by this calm, cultivated man of science of Indians, Mormons, mountaineers, and prairie life ring somewhat differently in our ears from similar accounts written by American or even English observers. His interest was naturally very strong in the natural history of all the regions he saw as in the scientific instruments and gadgets which he encountered. His descriptions of geological formations and specula-

[4] *Ibid.*, 138–47. See too Baldwin Möllhausen, *Diary of a Journey from the Mississippi to the Coasts of the Pacific.*

[5] Dr. John Evans, for example, was entrusted with the geological reconnaissance of Oregon for the Isaac Stevens expedition of 1853.

tions about their origin, his interest in methods of measuring distance and altitude, and his attempts to identify and classify the flora and fauna he saw make this unusual among European travel books about the Old West.

Some of the observations which Schiel made about the western landscape show a deep insight into the natural and cultural forces which were shaping the destiny of the country. He prophesied that future generations of Americans would see the buffalo only in museums for at the rate of their destruction, he noted in 1853, they could not avoid extermination within fifty to sixty years. He was quick to see, too, that what had been described on maps he had seen as the Great American Desert had no more resemblance to a real desert such as the Sahara than a bear to a camel.

A touch of German national pride (if it is proper to speak of a national pride among Germans in the 1850's) is revealed in an occasional comment, although the account is generally quite objective in this respect. He seems to have respected and liked his American companions, although he comments in one instance on the scientific incompetence of one of the meteorological experts at the Smithsonian Institution. His admiration for the mountaineer and Leatherstocking type seems to have known no bounds as is evident in his almost worshipful descriptions of the activities of the guides Massalino and Leroux. One humorous instance of national pride on Schiel's part is the proud revelation which he makes to his German countrymen that he had found only three Germans in the Mormon settlements of Utah.

Some of Schiel's sharpest barbs are aimed at the Mormons. His account of them is a curious combination of objective details mixed with unsympathetic reporting. The hyperbole and exaggeration common to most Westerners at this time is singled out for special ridicule in the Mormons. Polygamy he finds especially odious and ungenerously warns his countrymen considering emigration to Utah that he found not a single beautiful woman, or one approaching it, in all of the territory. He cannot even bring himself to admire their accomplishments in transforming their arid homeland into a thriving commonwealth, likening their achievements in this respect unfavorably to the Californians.

By the time the expedition reached Salt Lake City, the famous massacre of Captain Gunnison and his small party by Indians had taken place. The expedition had divided up at the end of October, 1853, in order to accelerate the work in the face of an oncoming winter. Shortly afterward, the main body of the expedition under Lieutenant Beckwith received word of the Indian attack and the death of Captain Gunnison with seven of his companions. Gunnison was a West Pointer and a seasoned campaigner, having accompanied Stansbury on his western survey in 1849, and had written a competent book about the Mormons as a result of a prolonged winter's stay in Salt Lake City.[6] Killed with Gunnison were three soldiers, a guide, an unidentified civilian, the German botanist Creutzfeldt, and the artist Richard Kern. The last two were likewise veterans of previous western exploration trips, Creutzfeldt having accompanied Frémont on his 1848 expedition and Kern, one of three well-known brothers engaged in western exploration and art work, having gone on several expeditions.[7]

[6] John W. Gunnison, *The Mormons*. Hubert Howe Bancroft described Gunnison's book in 1890 as "one of the most valuable and impartial works yet published by a gentile writer." *History of Utah*, 464.

[7] The most detailed and apparently most complete account of the massacre is Josiah F. Gibbs, "Gunnison Massacre—1853," *Utah Historical Quarterly*, Vol. I, 67–75.

Schiel's book, which has been unknown heretofore to students of the West, gives a new source of information about the circumstances of the massacre as well as other new information about the expedition. Schiel himself found and aided one of the survivors of the massacre after having been forced to drop out of the rescue party under Captain Morris when his horse gave out. The picture of this inexperienced foreign scientist being left alone with his dead horse in a barren wasteland near the scene of an Indian massacre is one of the most amusing in the book, although Schiel doubtless did not find it so. In true frontier fashion, Schiel finally took his rifle, strapped on a revolver, stuffed his pockets with ammunition, and was on his way back to camp.

Schiel paints a convincing picture of the monotony of life on the prairie for the sophisticated European. For a few weeks, he writes, the effects of a carefree life in the open, the bracing climate, and the ruggedness of the primitive mode of life combine to provide an exhilaration of the senses and spirit. "But when the stay is prolonged, when habit has taken the charm from the novel, and even interest in natural history must go almost completely unsatisfied, then the monotony of the prairie becomes palpable indeed. One grows tired of the eternal grass and celebrates the day when he sees the gigantic summits of the Rocky Mountains for the first time almost like a holiday." (p. 29)

The Gunnison expedition had been charged with exploring the so-called central route between the 38th and 39th parallels. The party left camp near Westport, Missouri, on June 23, 1853, following the Santa Fé Trail between the Osage and Kansas rivers. By July 16, the expedition had reached Fort Atkinson, where it was visited by a throng of Comanches who wanted to trade horses. Passing Bent's Fort, they ascended the Huerfano River and crossed over the Sangre de Cristo Pass, descending by a circuitous route along the Sangre de Cristo Creek. They then climbed up to Coochetopa Pass (now Cochetopa) through the beautiful Sawatch Valley (now Saguache) and came down on the western slope by way of the Coochetopa to the Grand River Valley. The Green River was crossed on October 1, and the eastern base of the Wasatch Mountains reached by the twelfth of that month. The route then led through Wasatch Pass to the Sevier Valley, where Gunnison wrote: "On reaching this plain, a stage is attained which I have so long desired to accomplish: the great mountains have been passed and a new wagon road open[ed] across the continent—a work which was almost unanimously pronounced impossible, by the men who know the mountains and this route over them."[8]

Near the Mormon settlement of Fillmore the Indian massacre of Gunnison and his companions occurred on October 26, and the rest of the expedition went into winter quarters at Salt Lake City soon thereafter. It was here that Schiel had opportunity for several months to study Mormon life and institutions.

With Lieutenant Beckwith now in charge, the expedition set out once more on April 4 for a reconnaissance through Weber Cañon, South Pass, Echo Cañon, White Clay Creek, Black's Fork, Fort Supply, Henry's Fork, and return to Salt Lake City. There official instructions were received to make a reconnaissance along the 42nd parallel to the Pacific. Beckwith's route was south of those taken by Frémont (1846) and Stansbury to the Goshute Mountains, where he found a prac-

[8] *Reports of Explorations and Surveys to Ascertain the Most Practicable and Economical Route for a Railroad from the Mississippi River to the Pacific Ocean*, II, part 1, 70.

ticable pass into the Goshute Valley. From here he advanced through easy passes to the Humboldt River Valley, the best known route through the Great Basin to California.

The exploratory work of Gunnison and Beckwith, like that of the other railroad survey expeditions, helped very little in bringing agreement in Congress on the route for a transcontinental railroad. The Gunnison route, though stoutly championed by Thomas Hart Benton, was given scant support because of the great engineering problems encountered. Secretary of War Jefferson Davis concluded on the basis of recommendations by the corps of topographical engineers that "the difficulties of engineering and the cost of construction of this portion of the route from Coo-che-to-pa Pass to Sevier river, in the Great Basin, a distance of about 500 miles, would be so great that it may be pronounced impracticable."[9] Although Davis recommended the southernmost route, northern Congressmen and Senators could not be made to agree. Not until the Civil War, with the South out of the Union, was agreement finally reached on the building of a transcontinental road.

The forgotten role which Schiel played in this episode in American history is due to the extreme rarity of the German edition of this book. It has been virtually unknown to American scholars as only three copies of the book are known to exist in this country. Even in Germany the book is very rare and my own interest was drawn to it accidentally by an interest in German-American medical relations. I made the natural assumption that Schiel was a German physician when I learned that he had been surgeon to the Gunnison expedition while in America.

[9] *Report of the Secretary of War Communicating the Several Pacific Railroad Explorations*, I, part 1, 24.

In translating the book I have sought to find the most direct and clear English expressions consonant with readability and have not sought for a "literary" translation. The style presents considerable difficulties. As a scientific man with no special penchant for writing, Schiel is exceedingly repetitious in vocabulary and sentence structure. Furthermore, the book is written partly in diary form, partly as a narrative with no clear line of separation so that tenses tend to be thoroughly mixed. Evidently, too, Schiel's energies flagged toward the end of the journey as the day by day entries of the early section of the book give way to a very sketchy coverage of the last portion of the journey. In correcting Schiel's orthography, I have generally followed contemporary usage as reflected in the official report of the expedition. Schiel succeeded in wildly misspelling almost every Indian name which appears in the book. The illustrations used in this book are from the official report of the expedition (*Reports of Explorations and Surveys ... from the Mississippi River to the Pacific Ocean,* II).

I should like to offer public thanks to the several persons who have given me aid and encouragement in this project: Professor Karl Thieme and his assistant librarian at the Auslands- und Dolmetscherinstitut in Germersheim; Professor J. Steudel, director of the Institute of Medical History at Bonn; Professor Ray Alan Billington of Northwestern University; and the members of the staff of the University of Oklahoma Press. I owe a special debt of gratitude to helpful colleagues at the University of Omaha who gave me assistance with technical questions, especially John G. McMillan and Robert J. Trankle, and Miss Ellen Lord and her library staff, notably Marion R. McCaulley, who helped in a great number of ways. Finally, I should like to thank James Sorensen and Richard Barnhart for their help in preparing the material used in the map.

THOMAS N. BONNER

*Omaha, Nebraska*
*January 18, 1959*

*Contents*

*Illustrations*

Journey Through the Rocky Mountains
and the Humboldt Mountains to the Pacific Ocean

# Chapter I

## *The Great Western Prairie and the Rocky Mountain Region*

Of the various expeditions under orders from the United States government to explore the country from the Mississippi to the Pacific Ocean in the years 1853 and 1854, the one under Captain Gunnison had what was called the central route to explore. The instructions which had been given him by the Secretary of War in Washington read in part:

Under the 10th and 11th sections of the military appropriation act of March 3, 1853, directing such explorations and surveys as to ascertain the most practicable and economic route for a railroad from the Mississippi to the Pacific Ocean, the War Department directs a reconnaissance of the country from the Missouri across the prairie and an exact and detailed exploration of the pass in the Rocky Mountains in the vicinity of the headwaters of the Río del Norte along the Huerfano River to the San Luis Valley, and from there over the Coochetopa or some other suitable pass into the valley of the Green River and westward to the Vegas de Santa Clara and the Nicollet River; thence to Lake Utah and through the Timpanogos Valley and other passes and valleys of the Wasatch range, across Bear and Weber rivers through the Coal basin to Fort Laramie.

Competent persons will be selected to make researches in those

3

River
Blue River
Robideau's Old Fort
Cochetopa Pass
Huerfano R.
Bent's Fort
Arkansas
Bent's Trading Post
Huerfano Butte
Sangre de Cristo Pass
Ft. Atkinson
Coon Creek
Pawnee Fork
Walnut Creek
Smoky Hill River
Kansas River
Westport
River
Wakarusa Bottoms
Uniontown
Missouri
River

ROUTE OF
Gunnison ~ Beckwith Expedition
1853 ~ 1854

0     100     200     300
MILES

branches of science which contribute to the solution of the question of location, construction, and support of a railway communication across the continent, viz: exploration of the nature of the rocks and soil and the products of the country, animal, mineral, and vegetable. Magnetic and meteorological, hygrometrical and electroscopical observations shall be made, together with astronomical observations for determining geographical points, so that the character of the land traversed will be well understood.[1]

It is easy to imagine that the preparations for a journey which would presumably take several summers and extend several thousand miles through regions inhabited only by Indian tribes, if at all habitable, would require considerable time. Nevertheless, after the custom of the country, everything went swiftly. Scarcely fourteen days had elapsed after receipt of the War Department order when the expedition, fully equipped and provided with everything needed, such as provisions, tents, etc., moved into camp near Westport on the western boundary of Missouri. In equipping and provisioning the expedition, it had to be considered that the instructions received could undergo a change during the campaign itself. It was by no means improbable that after we had explored the Wasatch Mountains, the Coal Basin, and the upper Green River region, we would be ordered by Washington to continue the exploration of the country as far as the Pacific Ocean. This was indeed what actually happened.

In order to bring convincing evidence to bear on the practicability of the route for the construction of a railroad, it was decided to load the equipment of the expedition on a number

[1] These instructions differ slightly from those cited in the official report. Nothing is said in the latter about a reconnaissance of the prairie country west of the Missouri, already well explored, although the expectation of confirmatory observations could well be implied. There are several minor differences in detail and spelling. *Reports of Explorations and Surveys*, II, part 1, 10.

of strong wagons like those used by the emigrants to California. A considerable number of saddlepacks were taken notwithstanding, so that in an emergency the wagons could be left behind. We needed the saddlepacks in any case for the frequently very extensive side trips away from the main route and for mountainous regions where wagons could not make the grade.

In the camp near Westport we had to spend an entire week in getting completely ready for the trip. Mules for the wagons and a number of riding-horses for the scientific corps had to be purchased. The majority of the former were still wild and untrained and had to be put through their first training, which is called the "breaking in" of the animals. During this time everyone was able to arrange his things as he needed them for field use. A quantity of medicines which I selected at the government supplier's in St. Louis was carefully packed in the chests of a wagon with springs, so that we were provided with a rather convenient traveling dispensary. The surrounding area was explored geognostically and the instruments for the various observations and surveys tested and adjusted. In this way it was possible to get somewhat used to camp life in advance, which up to now still retained something of the blessings of civilization, as nearby Westport was still delivering fresh meat and potatoes. Later we had to go without both for a long time as we spent long months in regions where scarcely a single bird was to be found and no hunter could provide us with fresh meat. Our provisions consisted of bread, rice, barley, and sides of bacon. Instead of nourishing peas and beans the commissariat officer from some odd whim had brought along a large quantity of dried apples, doubtless with the good intention of protecting us from scurvy.

The instruments for finding astronomical and geographical position consisted of two rather large sextants with attached artificial horizons (mercury horizon), one theodolite, and one telescope in addition to two chronometers, one of which was a Troughton box chronometer, the other a pocket chronometer. Some excellent compasses from the Schmalcalder[2] factory in Philadelphia served for the surveying of detail in the topographical work. In addition there were two Bunten barometers for measuring altitude—two aneroid barometers soon proved unreliable for the same purpose—and some thermometers and hygrometers on hand.[3] Two of the thermo-barometers, or thermometers which were supposed to determine altitude from the boiling point of water, had been damaged in shipment and, unfortunately, could not be used. The third one could be used only at altitudes under 4,000 feet above sea level, and with this I occasionally made some determinations which spoke favorably for the practical use of the instrument. Since, however, we found ourselves below this elevation only on the very first and last days of the trip no decisive results could be gained with this instrument.

In order to eliminate errors in the barometric level due to changes in the condition of the atmosphere during the time between readings, I suggested to Captain Gunnison that he have observations made simultaneously in two places, and at his wish I took over the direction of the meteorological and hypsometric work for the first few weeks.[4] It was clear that

[2] Schiel has given it the Germanic spelling of Schmalkalden.

[3] This account of the scientific equipment taken on the expedition varies at several points from the official report. See *Reports of Explorations and Surveys,* II, part 1, 12.

[4] There is no mention anywhere in the official report of Schiel's having been assigned this responsibility. He was doubtless very familiar with all kinds of scientific instruments, yet it seems a little curious that it is not mentioned either in the general report by Lieutenant Beckwith or in the separate discussions of meteorology and altitudes.

when the position of the barometer is observed at five o'clock in the morning at one camp and again after a march of some twenty miles and the passage of six to ten hours no reliable results relative to the differences in elevation can be obtained. Not only may the condition of the atmosphere change significantly during this time but also it is not known positively whether this change has extended uniformly over the entire distance. The observations were therefore undertaken in such a way that one of two observers went several miles ahead with one instrument and the other remained behind with the second barometer to observe the level of the instrument simultaneously with the first at an agreed time. The one who went ahead designated the place where he had observed each time with a pennon, so that the one following found the places where he was to repeat his observations. According to the locality and other circumstances, observations were taken every hour or at shorter time intervals. The observer who stayed behind got a security guard of a dozen soldiers, all of them mounted riflemen. In this fashion three sets of observations could be obtained and mistakes and errors excluded as much as possible. We obtained the differences in altitude not only from the barometric level of each instrument measured against itself but also from the simultaneous difference in the two instruments and could thus control the one by the other. The greater reliability of this method was impaired, however, when a second pair of the Bunten barometers, which were supposed to be sent on to the expedition at Westport, failed to appear because their carrier became sick en route.[5] One of the Buntens on hand had too slow an action and was not at all

---

[5] The man bringing them was a civil engineer engaged by Gunnison for the expedition who fell sick before reaching St. Louis. *Reports of Explorations and Surveys,* II, part 1, 12.

reliable. Unfortunately, therefore, the method soon had to be limited in its application, especially since no help in the procedure was to be expected from the aneroid barometers.

Since we did not know exactly what barometric level corresponded to the median sea level between ebb and flood-tide, I suggested to Mr. Blodget[6] in Washington that variations in altitude be drawn relative to an imaginary sea level corresponding to the barometric level of 30 inches and 0 degrees. This he did with the help of tables published by the Smithsonian Institute, but the considerations which entered into his computations show that the mathematical and physical theories of the modern era are not clear to him.

Whoever journeys from Westport on the western boundary of Missouri toward the Rocky Mountains between the Kansas and the Arkansas will be struck after a few days travel by the poverty of the great western prairie in trees and shrub-like vegetation. This prairie differs not altogether advantageously from the region east of the Mississippi. Woodland and brushwood cover considerable stretches of the latter and are often found also in scattered islands on the prairies, but on the western or great prairie such vegetation is found only on the banks of rivers and streams, and even there it never stretches out to any significant extent. In the states of Ohio, Indiana, Illinois, and even in Missouri, the population is not at a loss for wood but in the future states of Kansas and Nebraska, especially in the western part, this lack will become very ap-

[6] Lorin Blodget (1823–1901), statistician, climatologist, and publicist was put in charge of researches in climatology at the Smithsonian Institution in 1851. During 1852–1856 he was employed by the War Department for the Pacific Railroad survey and directed the determinations of altitudes and gradients by the use of the barometer. His book, *Climatology of the United States* (J. B. Lippincott and Co.), published in 1857, was the first work of importance on the climatology of any part of America. *Dictionary of American Biography,* II, 379.

Wah-ha-ta-gas or Spanish Peaks from near the Cuchara, August 6.

View of Sangre de Cristo Pass looking northeast from camp north of summit, August 11.

parent in time if the coal deposits found there do not offer a partial substitute for wood. What the cause of this break in the vegetation of that region is is difficult to say. Many travelers believe they have found it in the innumerable buffalo herds and the frequent prairie fires which trample and burn up the young tree-shoots; but it is a fact that the land from the Missouri to Walnut Creek,[7] a distance of almost 270 English miles, where for thirty years only a few buffaloes have been encountered, is extremely poor in wood while forests and shrubbery flourish in regions where prairie fires are not a rare occurrence. A more reliable explanation of the phenomenon can be expected only from a thorough observation and examination of the climatic relations, the soil, and other possible influences but nevertheless the appearance of a rather luxuriant tree growth on the damp river banks speaks for the view that buffalo herds and prairie fires will not do as a sufficient explanation of this peculiar phenomenon.

The journey over the almost endless ocean of grass from Missouri to the foot of the Rocky Mountains takes over a month if the pack animals are not to be ruined by extreme exertion and made unfit for the more difficult service in the mountains. An average day's march of twenty English miles[8] is an achievement which with the small rise of the terrain does not hurt the animals. The western prairie is a sloping plain which ascends gradually and, if barometric aids are not used, almost unnoticeably from the Missouri to the Rocky Mountains. While Westport lies only 995 feet above sea level, the base of the mountains opposite the Spanish peaks is over 7,400 feet above the Gulf, but the distance is nearly 700 miles so

[7] Flows into the Kansas near the 98th degree of longitude.—J. H. S.

[8] By mile I understand in the following the English mile of 1,765 yards [*sic*] or 5,280 feet.—J. H. S.

that the rise of the terrain amounts to an average of not more than ten feet to the mile. Citing the altitudes and distances of some of the more important points will make this relationship clear.

| | Altitude above sea level in English feet | Distance from Westport in English miles |
|---|---|---|
| Westport | 990 | |
| Walnut Creek | 1,960 | 269 |
| Coon Creek | 2,240 | 318 |
| Bent's Fort | 3,670 | 559 |
| Apishpa, on the map erroneously cited as Huerfano* | 4,723 | 608 |
| Huerfano, at the mouth of the Arkansas | 6,090 | 673 |
| Foot of the Spanish Peaks | 7,460 | 696 |

* The reference is presumably to one of the maps used by the expedition, which included those made by Nicollet, Stansbury, and Frémont, the land office surveys of Missouri, and the Pacific Coast survey maps. No maps were included in the German edition of Schiel's book. —editor's note.

The distances given were measured by an instrument frequently used by the so-called "Overlanders," as the travelers on the road to California are sometimes called. It has received the name odometer (from *odos*, path). The instrument is as simple as it is clever and consists of a brass case with cover about nine or ten centimeters in diameter and five or six centimeters high. It is fastened in a protective leather cover to a spoke of one of the rear wagon wheels so that the diameter of the instrument lies in the direction of the spoke, i.e. in a vertical plane. In the case is a circle divided up into sections of ten

gradations each over which two pointers move, the one showing the separate rotations of the wheel, the other the number
of rotations in hundreds. The pointers are moved by a gear
arrangement which is connected with a plumb-bob hanging
from a horizontal peg (axis) in the middle of the case. Since
the plummet line moving around the axle always retains its
vertical position, while the peg along with the whole instrument completes a circular movement with each rotation of the
wheel, here is a simple means of moving the gearing and
thereby the pointers. If the circumference of the wheel to
which the instrument is fastened is exactly measured, the distance covered is known from the number of revolutions of
the wheel.[9]

The journey from Westport to Walnut Creek, where the
real buffalo region begins, passes through Council Grove,[10]
which only a few years ago was a trading post and rest-stop for
the caravans going to Santa Fé but is now one of the outposts
of the state of Kansas.[11] The settlement is located in a pretty
little wooded area on Neosho Creek and possesses a rather
large tract of cultivated land of excellent quality. We met
here the governor of New Mexico, Merriwether,[12] who was
on his way to Santa Fé. Thirty years ago he sat as a prisoner
in the same palace which he is now to occupy as governor of

[9] Apparently the Mormons were the first to use this ingenious device. See
the discussion and explanation of its working in Leland H. Creer, *The Founding
of an Empire*, 276–77.

[10] Spelled Cuncil Grove in the original.

[11] The party divided at Bull Creek, Dr. Schiel traveling with Lt. Beckwith
along the Santa Fé road and part of the expedition going with Captain Gunnison
along the Kansas River in a parallel course twenty to thirty miles north as far
as Walnut Creek. *Reports of Explorations and Surveys*, II, part 1, 13–23.

[12] David Meriwether, governor of New Mexico territory from 1853 to
1857, was a Democratic politician and long-time member of the Kentucky
legislature. He served briefly by appointment in the United States Senate in 1852.
*Appletons' Cyclopaedia of American Biography*, IV, 304.

the state [i.e. territory]. At that time he was engaged in trade with the Indians and accompanied a band of Pawnee warriors on a war march to New Mexico. The Indians, however, ventured too far into the interior of the country. They were all wiped out by the Mexicans in a battle and the future governor of the state with his attendant was held prisoner for a long time.

After a fourteen-day trip we made camp on the ninth of July on Walnut Creek, which flows into the Smoky Hill Fork of the Kansas River[13] near 98° longitude and 39° latitude. We found camped here a dirty army of Kansas, Osage, Kaw, and Sac Indians, whose hunters were hunting buffalo. They were an indescribably greasy, degenerate people full of vermin, and we had a great deal of trouble guarding against their forwardness and begging, which because of the latter condition were dangerous. Although the real buffalo region begins here and the animals as a rule are found here in innumerable herds, we saw only isolated examples at this time. Only on the following day after a march of twenty-one miles did we find the prairie covered with herds of the ungainly giants, and that much-praised delicacy, fresh buffalo tongue, became a common sight at our meals.

In several other respects Walnut Creek is a remarkable point on the high prairie. Fort Atkinson was moved here by the central government from farther west because the locality is better suited to the purpose of the fort, which is supervision of the tribes and protection of the Santa Fé road. The banks of the stream, which is about twenty to thirty feet wide and up to three feet deep, are rather thickly overgrown with elms, ashes, and cottonwood trees, most of which, however, have a

[13] This is not true. At its closest point Walnut Creek is about fifteen miles distant from the Smoky Hill Fork.

short gnarled trunk and are suited only for firewood. And yet this vegetation seems luxuriant in comparison to that which is seen from now on on the prairie. The soil from here on becomes worse and worse and increasingly sandy and supports almost nothing except the short buffalo grass (*Sesleria dactyloides*). Wood becomes so scarce that it is often necessary to prepare meals with dry buffalo chips.

We encountered a national plague here in the mosquitoes, which went beyond everything that we had experienced or read of these insects anywhere, even the mosquito coast, which we were to see later, not excepted. The air was entirely filled with the little things, and when in the evening we slaughtered and skinned one of the oxen bought from the Indians, it became black instantaneously with the mosquitoes which literally covered it. In order to have at least a few hours rest from them overnight, it was necessary to build little fires in front of the tents, then conduct the smoke from the fresh wood and damp grass into the tent and keep it closed up until one wanted to lie down. In addition to this, a mosquito net had to be hung over the front end of the tent and over its inhabitant. But despite all this trouble and precaution, some of the little bloodthirsty monsters always found some opening through which they could reach their victims and plague them.

We became acquainted here for the first time with another annoyance which the traveler on the prairie encounters, a plague of a more serious character, in *Rhus toxocodendron* and *Rhus typhina* poisoning, both very widespread in this region.[14] The poison of these plants does not strike everyone with equal effect. Many were not at all susceptible to the poison, some on the contrary were so susceptible that they became infected just

[14] *Rhus toxocodendron* is poison ivy, but *Rhus typhina* is a non-poisonous sumac according to specialists in botany whom I have consulted.

from being in the vicinity of these plants. The worst case was the young astronomer of the expedition, Sheppard Homans, for despite the scrupulous caution with which he avoided all such bushes, he was seriously poisoned on several occasions. The symptoms of the poisoning are dizziness, headache, nausea, and a blister-like eruption which often spreads over the entire body, neck, arms, and legs and becomes very painful. Lacking a soft hospital bed in the camp, the victim can neither stand, sit or lie down without feeling great pain. There is nothing for him to do but bear his fate with the best possible composure. Fortunately the illness is not obstinate and yields quickly when the affected parts are washed over several times a day with a little sponge saturated with a very diluted solution of corrosive sublimate. Internally a gentle laxative and some lemonade as a beverage were sufficient in most cases to complete the cure. In time the organism seems to build up resistance against the operation of the poison. When we crossed the Arkansas fourteen days later by means of a raft and were forced by the approaching darkness to spread our buffalo skins on beatendown brush that was strongly shot through with *Rhus*, not a single case of poisoning came to my attention. Even H. [Homans], fully recovered only two days before, withstood the proximity of these plants so dangerous to him earlier without feeling the slightest injurious effect.

In order to give a clear, vivid picture of life on the high prairie, I am going to include some excerpts from the diary which I kept during our stay in the wilderness but here and there I will combine the notes of several days so as not to fatigue with less interesting details. I begin with the day when we had our camp on Coon Creek, a small stream which flows into the Arkansas about 337 miles west of Westport.

*July 15.* A magnificent badger was shot very near the camp this morning and was skinned for the collection.[15] We had hardly left our camp when our attention was arrested by a most interesting spectacle. Not more than several hundred paces from our wagon train a wolf was chasing a rabbit which by a thousand zig-zags, crosses, and bounds sought to elude his rapacious pursuer and arrive at his burrow. He succeeded in this, but when he got to the burrow he found a second wolf, apparently posted here by agreement with the first. The doubly-pursued rabbit succeeded, nevertheless, in enticing both of the savage animals away and escaping into his hiding-place. It was a splendid defense maneuver the little thing had executed in its own way, and it won the applause and good wishes of us all. The physiognomies of the two wolves were comical to see as they slunk away with their disappointed expectations.

One of our lads caught a live rattlesnake in the afternoon, a dangerous art in which he seemed to possess some skill. He had grasped it quickly with one hand close behind the head and the other at the rattles and the animal seemed to submit quietly to its fate. Since I did not know anything better to do with the snake, I tested the effectiveness of chloroform on it, of which a considerable supply was on hand. A cotton pad moistened with chloroform, which I held with pincers before the animal, brought about complete narcosis in less than half a minute. Loops were now put around his neck and rattles and he was tied in a horizontal position with very little room for movement. He recovered after a few minutes and tried to escape. A repeated chloroforming, possibly continued for two

[15] According to Beckwith's report, the animal "was too much injured for preservation." *Reports of Explorations and Surveys*, II, part 1, 24.

minutes, brought death to the animal which led a humorous Irishman, assistant to our astronomer, to conclude that chloroform could not be used when pulling the teeth of rattlesnakes.

*July 16.* After a day's march of about twenty miles we are camping on the Arkansas. On the other side of the river is a large camp of Comanches. A large herd of stately horses and mules, all duly acquired in the Comanche fashion, is grazing on the banks of the river, which is unusually high for the present season. They had posted a number of squaws as sentinels on this side of the river, and when we passed them, we were soon surrounded by a crowd of men, women, and children. Some of the chiefs formed a corps of honor which escorted us to our camping place. The courtesy of our normally dangerous companions is explained simply by the circumstance that they are awaiting an agent of the central government, who is on the way with presents for the tribes. Men, women, and children cross over the river in crowds and annoy us with their attentions. Among the children were two boys recognizable immediately as typical of the Anglo-Saxon race; they had blond hair and blue eyes and had very probably been kidnapped from a Texan settlement, although the Indians assured us that they had found them helpless on the prairie where their parents had died. One might have sworn that the boys were of German descent, but they understood only the language of the Comanches and a few words of Spanish, and nothing could be found out from them concerning their parentage since they remembered nothing themselves.

Just as we sat down to the noon meal the head chief of the Comanches, Shaved Head, honored us with a visit accompanied by some of his braves and chiefs. Shaved Head commands some thousands of mounted Comanche warriors, some say ten thousand, and he seems fully conscious of his importance and dignity. He is of majestic build, his bearing is serious and grave, and his behavior is almost ceremonious. Some blankets were spread out upon which he and his companions sat down. The peace pipe was smoked, and they were given something to eat. They all partook valiantly, and what they could not manage to eat they put aside to take with them as is customary with them. Of special interest was the departure ceremony which he conducted with all he considered worthy of attention and took to be a chief. It went as follows: Shaved Head grasps the right hand of the white chief forcibly in his, looks him fast in the eye, and shakes his hand three times, slowly, gravely, and ceremoniously; then he releases the hand, entwines his right arm in the right arm of the white chief's so that both are facing in opposite directions, and thrusts the other's elbow into his side three times, likewise in a slow tempo, during which he cries out "bueno, mucho bueno" each time. The same maneuver was repeated on the left side, and after the last thrust, Shaved Head released the arm, turned around, and marched off gravely with his following without looking around or taking notice of anyone.

Opposite our camp but on this side of the river is a camp of the Kioway Indians which shelters only their old men, wives, and children. Their warriors have joined in a campaign with the Cheyennes, Arrapahoes, Jicarilla Apaches, and a band of Comanches to wipe out the Pawnees. Their wigwams are very miserable, consisting chiefly of a few poles and some loose brush, and they contrast unfavorably with the lodges of the Comanches, in whom one recognizes the well-being of the accomplished thief. As I was returning in the afternoon from a little excursion and went through their camp, I passed a half-dozen papooses who appeared to be playing on the ground. I held out my hand to one of them, but they all ran away howling in terror of the white man. I was immediately surrounded by a crowd of half-naked squaws all cackling excitedly. From their gestures, they were giving me a thorough scolding, but since I understood no Kioway, I could not ask the ladies' pardon and had to laugh at the comical situation. I went on my way to give them a chance to arrange their toilets, which seemed very neglected in every respect.

Today we had beautiful proof of a kind I had never seen before of the existence of different air currents in different layers of atmosphere. I was resting on a wool blanket in the shade of my tent when Captain Gunnison passed by and directed my attention to two little clouds which hung like two cotton flakes in the otherwise clear blue sky. One came from the South, the other from the North, and they might have been some forty degrees away from each other at the time I saw them. It was a surprising sight to see how they slowly approached and passed close by each other and gradually were lost from view in opposite directions on the horizon.

We were able to enjoy fully the buffalo hunt today as for several days past. The animals were hunted with all sorts of weapons, with arrow, rifle, and pistol, on foot and on horseback. Hunting on horseback with a pistol, preferably a six-shot revolver called a *six-shooter*, is surely the most wonderful hunting pleasure that one can imagine, but it requires a good, fast, and maneuverable horse, a steady hand, and a sturdy rider. The hunter picks out one of the last bulls in a wandering herd, rides up to him, and when he turns aside, usually forces him from the herd. He tries to come at him from the left side, rides up close alongside of the fleeing animal, and seizes him sharply behind the left shoulderblade. For a few short minutes hunter and buffalo thunder in mortal proximity over the prairie, then comes a light press of the finger, and the shot is fired. The colossal bull still makes a few leaps and plunges; the hunter flies by to return to his prey with a round from the left. The fatally wounded animal dies quickly, and the hunter usually takes as reward for his bloody deed only the tongue, which he skillfully cuts off from underneath at the root. At most he takes the hump. The rest falls to the wolves or is left to putrefy and decompose.

Not always does the buffalo hunt run so smooth a course, however. If the buffalo is poorly hit, he sometimes turns on the rider, who then has a plentiful opportunity to show his skill or else suffer a severe blow as was actually the case this morning with one of the two young gentlemen from St. Louis who accompanied us into this region because of the hunt. He got too near a bull and the horse, which had not been broken in on the hunt, came too far forward. Before the hunter could shoot the buffalo bore down with his left horn, struck him on the leg, and hurled him out of the saddle. The frightened horse ran into our camp and to the great relief of everyone he was followed a half hour later by the rider, who fortunately escaped this time with simple shock and torn trousers. Another danger, which can be worse when the hunter forgets it in the excitement of the hunt, lies in the fact that the ground of the prairie is so undermined in many places by gophers or rats and here and there by badgers as well that a galloping horse sometimes breaks through, falls, and with his rider rolls to the ground. If the rider has not broken a leg, an arm, or even his neck and escapes with only bruises, his enjoyment of the hunt has been unusually pleasant and happy.

Future generations will know the buffalo only from museum examples and the descriptions of natural historians and the buffalo hunt only from the portrayals of travelers, for it can be predicted with considerable probability that in fifty or sixty years the species will have completely disappeared if treated as at present. The buffalo region is not a very wide strip, and it takes only a few days to ride through it in an east-west direction. It is regarded by the Indians as neutral ground, and in summer the tribes camp on the eastern and western boundaries of the region to hunt. The Sacs, Osage, Kansas, Pawnees, and other tribes camp to the east while on the west side the Kioways, Comanches, Cheyennes, Arrapahoes, and tribes related and friendly to them make their contribution to the extermination of the animals compressed into this confined space. The destruction of the buffalo is for the Indian synonymous with suicide. One may accept the view that the red man is incapable of civilization as an unhappy fact or regard it as a matter of humane doubt but so much is certain: he is and has been until now chiefly dependent upon the buffalo for his subsistence, and he must live and go down with him. The buffalo seems as little capable of domestication as the Indian has been won over to civilization. I have often heard assurances that in the swampy parts of southern Missouri hybrids of buffalo and the domestic breeds of the region still exist and are marked by such unusual wildness that no one may go near them.

*July 25.*   We made an unsuccessful attempt today to procure some live prairie dogs. A considerable number of them were in the vicinity of our camp. Neither the pouring of a large quantity of water into their burrows nor digging for them brought success. The burrow of each animal consists of a great number of branches and is probably connected with that of his neighbor which accounts for the rapid sinking of the water into the ground. When they are being chased, moreover, they dig new passages or extend the old ones with great speed. When they cannot escape, they prefer, it seems, to die in the flood which comes over them so suddenly and unexpectedly and against which they have made no provision. An owl is frequently seen sitting as a sentry on the mound formed around the entrance of the prairie dog's burrow by the dirt thrown out of the hole. This seems to confirm the popular opinion that prairie dogs, owls, and rattlesnakes live in one and the same burrow. In innumerable cases, however, I never found one of these owls inside of the burrow or saw one coming out or slipping in, apart from the fact, as might be expected, that they are always seen flying away as one approaches the burrow or shoots at it. It is completely true, however, that the rattlesnake, when it is trying to escape pursuit, frequently takes refuge in a prairie dog's burrow. It does not go to the bottom of the burrow, however, but stays close to the entrance. I have shot several snakes myself in this kind of refuge and pulled them out with a pronged stick. In one case, where the snake seemed very fat, it was shown on opening it that it had eaten not a young prairie dog but a gopher.

The prairie dog, which natural history knows as the American marmot and has named *Arctomys ludovicianus,* does not hibernate in winter like his European relative. Since he frequently lives in regions which are extraordinarily desolate and barren it would cost him considerable labor to lay in a winter's supply. They are extraordinarily alert, and when one approaches a burrow or a community of them, they all retreat with a few comical movements which look almost like preparations for defense. Only a little head is seen looking out over the mound of the next burrow and emitting a sharp whistling sound, which has not the least resemblance to the barking of a dog. When one comes to within sixty to eighty paces of the burrow the little head disappears and the whistling is heard in one or several of the nearest dwellings. We succeeded, nevertheless, in bringing down two of them for preservation with an excellent English double-barrelled gun which threw its shot an unusually long distance. One appeared completely unwounded. He had been only stunned by a grazing shot on the head, it seemed, had fallen across the entrance to the burrow, and gradually came back to life. The meat of the prairie dog has a loathsome taste, almost like butyric acid, and is absolutely unpalatable. I had the cook prepare one of them after the skin was removed, but it was not possible for any of us to enjoy a bit; the smell alone was enough to take one's appetite away.

*July 26.* Yesterday we left the so-called Big Timber of the Arkansas River behind us and today we passed by Bent's Fort.[16] The Big Timber is a rather thinly wooded section of poor cottonwood trees which grow on islands in the river and on its banks. It is about twenty miles long and earns its name only by comparison with the vegetation we have been seeing for several weeks. Creutzfeldt[17] found today the peeled-off skin of a seven-foot-long snake, which was so well preserved that one was tempted to believe that the animal had just shed

[16] Here, as at several points, Schiel's diary varies a day or two from the official account of the same events, due possibly to Schiel's having lost track of the date or to carelessness in running notes from several days together. According to Beckwith's official report, the party reached Big Timber on the twenty-sixth and Bent's Fort (actually a point three miles below) on the twenty-eighth. They passed by a vacant trading-station of Bent's on the twenty-seventh.

[17] F. Creutzfeldt, German botanist for the expedition. Of the many spellings of Creutzfeldt's name, I have used that in the official report. Schiel himself is not consistent, spelling it Creuzfeldt in one place and Kreutzfeld in another. The Gunnison massacre memorial near Deseret spells his name Creuzfeld. His first initial is given as J on the memorial, C by Schiel, and F in the official report. The problem arises from attempted Anglicization of a German name.

it a few minutes before. The horny cover of the eyes was completely preserved and the skin had the position as though the animal had just slid out through the opening of the jaws.

Bent's Fort has been abandoned by its owner, and its earthworks are for the most part ruined. There is naturally no trace of a roof to be found. The soil in the vicinity is hard and dry, yet the buffalo grass grows rather well here. The country has grown more forsaken, and the monotony of the prairie has become exceedingly wearisome since the nineteenth, when we quit our two-day camp at Fort Atkinson, very near 38° latitude and 100° 75′ [*sic*] longitude, and the Santa Fé road, which turns south there across the Arkansas. Forty miles west of the latter fort, the artemisia bush makes its appearance and reminds the traveler that he is approaching the so-called American desert. Only occasionally now does one see a helianthus, a thistle, or a geranium. The soil is often so hard that it rings under the horses' footsteps, and when putting up the tent, it is barely possible to drive a tent pole into the earth. The beginning of a new region for animal life is also indicated by the gradual disappearance of rattlesnakes, mosquitoes, and other pests and the appearance of huge locusts and the so-called horned frog (*Phrynosoma*), a lizard whose thick, elongated scales about the head take on the appearance of horns. Life in the tent again acquires something of comfort.

About three miles west of Bent's Fort, there begins a row of hills which extends some twenty miles west and from the approximately three hundred foot ridges one enjoys a view which is nothing less than serene. Their south slope is steep, almost perpendicular, and reveals two varieties of limestone in horizontal stratification, one over the other. The upper is white, hard, extremely fine-grained, and includes no fossil remains. The lower is brownish and interspersed with crystals of carbonate of lime; it shows traces of fossils, but they are so obliterated that they can no longer be recognized. It is hardly necessary for me to cite the frequent temptation to see a piece of the stem of an *Equisetum* in a chunk of sand broken off for the collection. Both varieties of limestone, which are supported by a blackish limestone and a soft shale, belong very probably to the cretaceous system which crops up unmistakably about ninety miles west of Fort Atkinson. It is represented by several limestones of which one is soft, argillaceous, yellow in color, and encloses an unidentifiable kind of oyster; another, which is gray and somewhat harder, could almost be described as a fossil bed of *Inoceramus*, so closely packed is it with a species which I named provisionally *Inocer pseudomytiloides* because of a bending out of the striae, which is not found in *Inocer mytiloides* according to the accounts of the paleontologists. The stratification of these limestones is likewise horizontal and concordant with that of the first described limestone at Bent's Fort. How far the cretaceous stretches to the north and south remains to be investigated.

Over the entire distance covered to this point there has been no occasion to challenge the well-known fact that the cretaceous system, where it appears in North America, rests on no more recent variety of rock than the members of the carboniferous system. From Westport to the Little Arkansas, a stream only about forty miles distant from Walnut Creek, the carboniferous is clearly recognizable from the characteristic fossils which are found locked in the stone. At Westport the gray limestone is almost nothing but a conglomerate of terebratula, spirifers, productus, and small, delicate trilobites.[18] Then follows a series of limestones changing in color and hardness which are characterized by *Fenestella, Productus*

[18] *Terebratula subtilita, Spirifer striatus, Productus splendens* and *Phillipsia.*—J. H. S.

26

Sangre de Cristo Pass from near the summit looking down Gunnison Creek.

Sangre de Cristo Pass looking towards San Luis Valley.

*semireticulatus,* and *Productus aequicostatus.* In many cases the organic enclosures are so obliterated by crystallization that their presence would not even be suspected if the surface of the stone, where exposed to the effect of running water, did not give the appearance that the remains had been strewn on top of it due to the gradual decomposition of the softer, uncrystallized pieces of limestone. This was the case among others with a yellowish limestone which I found on Indian Creek a few days journey from Westport. Its surface was covered with parts of broken stems of encrinites and fragments of bryozoa and small undistinguishable shells while the cleavage of the rock did not indicate anything like this. All of these limestones, which come to light only occasionally in the prairieland, have a slight declination to the northeast. It seems at times as if other rocks may lie between them. It is remarkable, however, that on the entire route the huge coal beds of this formation did not come to light.

Another phenomenon comes to mind here whose cause at first sight can and indeed has been misunderstood in similar cases, as I had occasion to realize. The limestones mentioned above as appearing west of Fort Atkinson form a low row of hills extending westward for a long way. On these hills are lines which might be taken for shore-lines marking the level of an ancient sea. They are, however, only the upper boundary of the limestone which lies in a horizontal position. The steep slope of the hills has certainly not been formed by a river or sea but through gradual wearing away by downpouring rain.[19]

About thirty-four miles west of Bent's Fort opposite the mouth of the Apishpa we had moved into camp on the twenty-

[19] Yet Schiel himself in his report on geology accompanying the official report had written of these same hills that they "show lines which mark the banks of an ancient sea." See, too, the accompanying note of Lt. Beckwith. *Reports of Explorations and Surveys,* II, part 2, 97.

ninth of August [*sic*]²⁰ to make preparations to cross the Arkansas above the mouth of the former river. It seemed as if all the reptiles in the neighborhood had gathered here in this broad bottomland to bid us farewell. Almost a dozen rattlesnakes were killed before the tents were put up. When one of the soldiers the following morning raised up his saddle, which as usual had served him as a pillow, he found beneath a coiled rattlesnake which paid with its life for its confidence in our hospitality. Upon examining my buffalo robe before lying down, I found in it no less than four scorpions of varying size. The largest was almost three inches long and the smallest three-quarters of an inch. I picked them up one after another with a long pincers which I carried in my pocket for such purposes and deposited them in alcohol. There was also a surplus of mosquitoes and large horseflies which tormented our horses and mules in the cruelest way. We had to spend several days here, for the Arkansas offered no convenient crossing in the entire region for the wagons, whose wheels were not very wide and consequently might cut too deeply into the sandy riverbed. Consequently a raft was built out of cottonwood trunks, and those objects which could not stand the water were gotten to the other side with great exertion and labor. The stream was not over 150 feet wide but very rapid and deep. One of the persons who undertook to swim to the other bank with one end of a rope was almost drowned. He had tied the rope to his left arm with a handkerchief in order to be able to swim better, but the current was so strong and drove him so swiftly downstream that he lost the use of this arm completely. He was saved only by the quick assistance of the others. After the wagons were freed from such a large part of their load, the passage could be effected farther up, where the river shrank

²⁰ The correct date seems to have been the twenty-ninth of July.

to a width of nine hundred feet and fell to a depth of not more than three feet. Even here the current was quite strong.

From the camp which we made August 1 on the right bank of the Arkansas, we saw for the first time that evening the Rocky Mountains standing beautiful and distinct before us. The Spanish Peaks and their northern neighbors, the Greenhorn Mountains, lay directly in front of us over the horizon and from a nearby hill James' Peak could be seen, its summit covered with snow. It was a joyful sight for the entire expedition, for the monotony of the prairie had become very wearisome to all of us. A sojourn on the prairie of only a few weeks has many pleasures. The carefree, untroubled life on one's own; the nomadic camp life of which a certain beneficial ruggedness is a part; the daily change of residence, which at the beginning brings much that is new and interesting; and the beneficial influence of the climate of the high prairie upon health all make it easy to do without beauty of landscape and the little comforts of life. But when the stay is prolonged, when habit has taken the charm from the novel, and even interest in natural history must go almost completely unsatisfied, then the monotony of the prairie becomes palpable indeed. One grows tired of the eternal grass and celebrates the day when he sees the gigantic summits of the Rocky Mountains for the first time almost like a holiday.

On the sixth of August we had our camp on the Cuchara, quite an important mountain stream about forty feet wide and several feet deep. It rises in a mountain in the vicinity of the northern Spanish Peaks and flows into the Huerfano, which carries its waters to the Arkansas.[21] From the adjoining hills

---

[21] Now called the Cucharas River, it rises in the Sangre de Cristo Mountains southwest of La Veta and flows seventy miles northeast past Walsenburg to the Huerfano River, twenty-five miles south of Pueblo.

we saw before us Pike's Peak to the north, while only a few miles away to the south and west, respectively, lay the Spanish Peaks and the Sierra Mojada in imposing masses.[22] The terrain, which had become more and more hilly after we left the Arkansas, flattens out toward the mountains into a broad, barren plateau. The soil is at times argillaceous, but the dominant rock is sandstone of a gray or red color, which is supported by a rather soft shale. Numerous rivers and creeks have dug beds through this rock, most of them enclosed by steep, perpendicular walls. These rivers are often so hidden from view that one is astounded to encounter strong rivers in a region where not one trace of water had been suspected. The Mexicans, as is well known, call such narrow canals enclosed by steep cliffs *cañons*, while they designate those with soft, earthy, or slatelike walls as *arroyos*.

The vegetation of this entire region presents a very miserable appearance. Here and there a wretched pine or a cottonwood tree are to be seen. Short, entwined cedars with widearching branches, on the other hand, are quite frequent and, during the heat of the day, provide welcome shade, for it is not uncommon for the temperature to reach 104° F. in the shade despite the altitude. The only examples of a somewhat more luxuriant growth are shrub-like cactus which sometimes reach a height of more than five feet here. Their angular branches covered with small needles are whorled around the trunk and branch out in the same pattern. Unfortunately, they

[22] In an oft-quoted passage, Captain Gunnison wrote of the same view: "Pike's Peak to the north, the Spanish Peaks to the south, the Sierra Mojada to the west, and the plains from the Arkansas—undulating with hills along the route we have come, but sweeping up in a gentle rise where we should have come—with the valleys of the Cuchara and Huerfano, make the finest prospect it has ever fallen to my lot to have seen." *Reports of Explorations and Surveys*, II, part 1, 36.

had already bloomed, and the calyxes of the blossoms hung from the juicy plants like tiny drinking-cups. Between the hills we always found grass enough for our animals, and the numerous herds of deer, antelope, and occasionally small herds of wild horses we met on our way prove that there can be no lack of grazing places in the entire region. Even the prairie dog seems to be very happy here, for innumerable packs of these animals are encountered on the plateau, although his prairie companions, the snake and the owl, have become a rarity. These are in general the characteristics of that stretch of land called the Great American Desert, which extends far to the south from the Black Hills along the Rocky Mountains in an average width of 100 to 120 miles and crosses over to the *Llano Estacado*. But the typical nature of this country resembles a real desert as little as the bear, the king of this desert, resembles the king of the African desert.

On the eighth of August we removed our camp to the vicinity of the Huerfano Butte,[23] close to the foot of the mountains. The Huerfano[24] Butte is an isolated cone of about 150 feet in height and visible from a great distance. It is made of black granite (quartz and mica) and a silicious slate found some miles to the east, where it is interspersed with a porphyritic rock. From this butte the Huerfano or Orphan River, which flows by no farther than a gunshot away, gets its name. The Huerfano is a rather swift-flowing mountain stream eighteen feet wide and one foot deep. It emerges from a narrow valley formed by the Sierra Mojada in the north and a spur of the Sierra Blanca in the south probably to flow into the Arkansas not more than twenty miles west of the Apishpa,

[23] From the French *butte*, hill.—J. H. S.
[24] Huerfano, an orphan.—J. H. S.

which is incorrectly designated as Huerfano on the maps.[25] Its banks are thickly overgrown with cottonwoods, wild plum, cherry, willow, and thorn-bushes, and everything takes on a fresher appearance in the immediate vicinity of the mountains. The soil in the neighborhood is quite light and could be made fertile with little effort through irrigation.

As we came close to the mountains we saw some grizzly bears that were walking around on the steep slope of the mountain and seemed to be watching us suspiciously. They were wonderful examples of bears, but they seemed to want no closer contact with us, and they were soon lost in the mountains. Since in the country through which we had recently come the bear was a rarity, these were the first specimens of these animals which we had had a chance to see.

At the foot of the Greenhorns is a little settlement of six families from New Mexico. They have several acres of land in cultivation on which they are planting corn, wheat, beans, and watermelon, and they also have a little herd of cows, horses, and mules. They make an excellent living meanwhile by hunting which is unusually rewarding here. One of our officers had gone with an escort of five men in search of the settlement to get information about the region and perhaps acquire a guide. He returned to camp yesterday with one of the settlers, Massalino, who will guide us into the San Luis Valley. According to the description, the houses of the settlement are built out of air-dried bricks or adobe and are without any windows or other openings except for a low door. In front of and behind each house is an open space twenty yards wide protected by a row of poles driven into the ground and lashed together with rawhide thongs. These yards are supposed to

[25] Again it is not clear to what maps Schiel has reference. See footnote at bottom of table, page 12.

serve as protection against the Utah Indians who the year before killed a part of their cows, destroyed their crops, and stole their horses. The houses, which with the exception of one are joined, are so low that a tall man can reach comfortably to the flat roof. This roof is the general assembly point when strangers approach the settlement and it is not known whether they are friend or foe. Massalino is by birth a New Mexican and about forty-five years old. He belongs to the dying race of Leatherstockings and has spent his entire life in the wilderness. He was by turns a hunter, trapper, voyageur, fighter, and guide and is familiar with the country as far as the Pacific Ocean. Because of the losses at the hands of the Utah Indians, he and his Pawnee wife recently removed to the Pueblo on the Arkansas where he and his family are the sole occupants. Here, too, he suffered misfortune. High water destroyed this year's little crop, and he and his family are now entirely dependent upon hunting for subsistence. "I once lived on meat alone for nine years," he said, "and can live well enough now from coffee and the game I shoot." He is reputed a fine hunter. "I never see a grizzly without trying a shot. I try to hit him in the right spot, but if I miss, I have to run. We will have some fun," he declared, pointing to the mountains. There are not many hunters bold enough to shoot at a grizzly bear unless accompanied by a well-armed companion. This formidable animal, able to haul away a buffalo between its front paws, is so tough that it is still dangerous to the hunter even when mortally wounded. The only way to kill him instantaneously, according to the testimony of the hunters, is to hit him in the nape of the neck so as to break his neck with the bullet.

*August 6.* We entered the mountains today. We crossed the Huerfano, went through a narrow ravine, and then followed a beautiful valley south which was a half-mile to a mile wide. It was formed from two spurs of the main chain of mountains. Countless helianthus, campanula, papilio flowers, and other plants are blooming in the luxuriant grass, and we moved literally on a beautiful, bright carpet of flowers.[26] Swarms of magnificent magpies encircled us from all sides but avoided our snares with great care. For the first time today I hunted a large grizzly discovered by one of the soldiers in a wooded part of the stream about fifty paces away. But before one of the hunters could get a shot, the bruin had run away and thereby spared the hunters the running, for it is a strict rule on these dangerous hunts that one of the participants, hunter or hunted, must run. After a distance of seven miles we had to put up our tents as it began to rain hard.

As we followed our southern direction the next morning, we came into a ravine through which a little brook flows north toward the Huerfano. The slope of the mountains was so steep that the wagons had to be held with ropes to prevent their overturning. The grass was so high here that it reached to the belly of the horses. We followed the brook for a little distance, opening a path through a forest of quaking asp with our axes. We tried to reach the summit of the Sangre de Cristo pass by turning left but had to put up our tents in a heavy rainstorm, this time on the slope of the mountain in a luxuriant field of grass and flowers. The mountains around us are covered with aspen and small pines although a fire swept over these mountains two years ago and destroyed much of the timber. This fire has left its traces on many trees in the blackened and burned bark.

[26] The same group of flowers in the official report is described as helianthus, verbena, lupine, and blue-flowering flax. *Reports of Explorations and Surveys,* II, part 1, 38.

A large part of our party was busy for two days clearing the forest to the peak of the mountain to make a passage by wagon possible. The trip over the pass was attended by many hardships. The wagons had to be dragged up one by one to be let down on ropes with no less effort on the other side of the pass. Because of the greatly rarified atmosphere stops had to be made every minute so that man as well as beast could rest and recover. Even though the number of mules per wagon was doubled to twelve on the summit of the pass, they could not accomplish what six mules could do under ordinary circumstances. Likewise, the achievements of our strongest men were reduced to less than half their normal performance.

While the wagon train was busy effecting a painful crossing of the Sangre de Cristo Pass, we had time to acquaint ourselves with the mountains in all directions and to investigate more thoroughly those depressions which might be suitable for the transit of a railroad. The novelty and adventurousness of the locality, the long-missed freshness of the vegetation, the grandeur and beauty of the scenery all made this investigation as pleasant as it was interesting. The tasty meal in the evening and relaxation by a blazing campfire made the day's work seem even less strenuous. We do not need to be so sparing of wood here as on the prairie for the sides of the mountains are overgrown with ashes and small pines, and they enclose many small, narrow valleys in whose soil a luxuriant grass grows. Game is at hand in unheard-of abundance. Grouse and pheasant abound, deer and bear are found in every valley and ravine, and the pretty mountain streams are filled with the finest trout.

Captain Gunnison and I rode northwest into the mountains early in the morning led by Massalino and escorted by eight soldiers to investigate a pass, until then known only to

hunters, which has a rise less steep than that of the Sangre de
Cristo Pass, according to our guide's assurances. We found the
guide's account confirmed, for this pass leads down gradually
to the Huerfano Valley at a steady decline from the mountain
ridge which joins it with the Sangre de Cristo Pass. As we
were about to cross a stream on this excursion, Massalino directed our attention by means of signs to an object on the other
side of the water. It was a magnificent white stag grazing
peacefully. He did not run until we had gotten within about
twenty paces of him. Massalino did not attempt to shoot and
seemed to regard him as a charmed beast. It seems as if the
animals in general in this part of the mountains are not familiar
with the danger from human beings. On the branch of a tree
which stretched out over a little grassy spot near this stream
there sat two plump pheasants thirty or forty paces away from
us as if waiting for a hunter who might like to shoot them.
Gunnison and I had already tried several shots with our re-
volvers without hitting either of them when Massalino dis-
mounted, aimed his long rifle, and shot off the head of one of
them. While I was tying the fallen bird to my saddle with
thongs, Massalino raised his rifle again and shot his comrade,
who seemed not in the least aware of the danger in the pro-
ceedings before him. The meat of these birds is unusually
tender and tasty, even if the appetite has not been sharpened
by a tiring excursion.

The thirteenth of August was bright and clear, and the
day's barometric observations could be used in determining
the elevation of the pass. It was computed at 9,396 feet above
sea level,[27] while the neighboring mountain peaks are close to

[27] Beckwith reports that the mean of the five hourly barometer observations
gave an altitude of 9,219 feet above sea level. *Reports of Explorations and Surveys,* II, part 1, 38.

ten thousand feet high. A little stream, El Sangre de Cristo, rises in the vicinity of the pass and flows in a southwesterly direction toward the San Luis Valley. The valley of the Sangre de Cristo is narrow and has many turns. The banks of the stream are thickly covered with willow bushes and for four days over a distance of five to six miles the entire force was busy making paths and crossings over the stream. During this time I again made an excursion with Captain Gunnison under Massalino's guidance, this time to investigate the mountains south of the Spanish Peaks. We rode up the valley of a stream which coalesced with El Sangre de Cristo Creek bearing the name "Gold Branch." This very winding valley gradually climbs at first in a northeasterly direction, then turns east and, after a mile, southeast. After a long, hard ride we climbed a high peak and from there enjoyed a magnificent view of the country which we had recently investigated. The Huerfano, Cuchara, and Apishpa flowed at our feet; to the north and south great mountain masses stretched toward heaven; to the west we had the San Luis Valley and beyond the colossal peaks of the Sierra San Juan towered on the horizon. The atmosphere was pure and transparent and allowed objects to be recognized clearly at a great distance. According to the barometer we were almost eleven thousand feet above sea level. Later we climbed still another mountain from which we could look down almost vertically upon the Cuchara. In climbing down, we came upon a very fresh trail made by a number of hunters who had come up from Taos. These people travel with horses and pack-mules on their hunts lasting about fourteen days and the return trip taking four days. The game is skinned and cut up, and in this condition it remains fresh during the entire time, although no trace of salt is used and rainstorms pour down almost daily around the highest mountain peaks. The only protection which the game requires is against flies, dogs, and wolves. The hunters, therefore, cover it with cloths during the day. At night they spread it out on the ground, lay their saddles on and between it, and sleep in their wool blankets among their treasures.

The main mountain mass, as far as we have come to know it until now, consists of a trachytic porphyry of bluish-gray, rough base in which a great number of feldspar and mica crystals are imbedded. The latter consist of regular, blackish, hexagonal leaflets which lie one upon the other in such profusion that the crystals form what one would be tempted to take for tourmaline crystals were it not for the easily identifiable cleavage of mica in the direction parallel to the end surfaces. This rock, which forms the mountain ridge from Sangre de Cristo Pass to the new pass mentioned above has a very changeable character. Beyond the cañon through which we entered the mountains, it is more gray, and the enclosed feldspar crystals are not glassy but ordinary white feldspar; west of the pass it is bluish-gray, the feldspar crystals diminish, and it is interspersed with a great number of small, black columns of tourmaline or hornblende. Significant quantities of a zeolitic substance called stilbite are not uncommon in this rock.

Of the stratified rocks I found only sandstone, which has been lifted only occasionally to the highest peaks of the mountains, and a red slate supporting it. At the entrance of the mountains the sandstone is white, fine-grained, hard, eroded and worn down, and almost vertically elevated by plutonic rocks. On only one occasion did I find it with a fifteen degree decline to the northeast. The steep slopes of the mountains are covered with fragments of a white silicate which often reach a considerable size and take the form of boulders twenty feet or more in diameter. The little hills at the base of the higher mountains are covered with boulders of all kinds, quartz, porphyry, sandstone, hypersthene, and others. Most or at least many of the summits have sharp, angular, bare ridges from which other ledges branch out laterally, giving the mountains a very strange appearance.

Granite crops out for the first time southwest of the pass in the Sangre de Cristo Valley and forms rugged groups on either side of the valley. This granite is very changeable in its appearance but it has one thing in common, that the mica it contains, whether yellow or white, possesses such a gold or silver luster that the belief arose among the men that we had found a new land of gold. On the right bank of the stream the granite passes successively into gneiss and hornblende rock— hornblende with a few grains of feldspar. On the gneiss lie shale, sandstone, and a blue-gray limestone which has fissured and disintegrated where it is exposed to the air. On the eastern side of the mountains a similar limestone appears. It is very probable that it belongs to the Lower Silurian system whose presence on the North American continent is definitely authenticated.

According to the testimony of our guide several streams in the mountains are supposed to contain gold. The name "Gold Branch Creek," which the mountaineers have given the stream mentioned above, shows that the belief is widespread in this region. We had already met a host of goldseekers on the prairie who were coming with a wagon train from Pike's Peak, where they had been vainly searching half the summer for gold, and were now returning to the States with their disappointed hopes and meager possessions. The possibility of the presence of gold in those regions cannot be discounted, of course, even though none of us succeeded in finding a trace of it. Yet I cannot overcome to this minute a strong doubt as to the presence of great quantities of gold in the vicinity of the peak.

The Sangre de Cristo Valley is not more than twelve to fifteen miles long and leads into the broad San Luis Valley. The latter is enclosed by two mighty mountain chains branching out from the three parks and extending in divided fashion to the south. Although these mountains have received a great many local names, they belong probably to not more than three different geological systems. The San Luis Valley is for the most part sandy and infertile. Artemisia bushes and several varieties of cactus, especially *Cactus opuntia*, make up the vegetation of this valley, which is watered by the Rio Grande del Norte with its numerous tributaries. Only in the narrow adjoining valleys situated higher where frequent rainstorms occur (which, curiously, rarely happens in wide valleys) is the vegetation fresh and luxuriant. In these adjoining valleys lie most of the ranches and villages of the New Mexicans. In leaving the Sangre de Cristo Valley, we crossed over a low ridge and came to a broad plain joining the San Luis Valley and reaching to the base of the Sierra Blanca. A march of less than eleven miles brought us to Fort Massachusetts which lies concealed at the foot of one of the snow-covered peaks of the Sierra so that one does not see it before he is upon it. The fort has a garrison of several hundred men whose assignment it is to hold in check the dangerous Taos Utahs, as the Utah Indians inhabiting the surrounding mountains are called. We stayed several days in camp in order to take on fresh provisions, shoe the horses, and have repairs made on the wagons and harnesses. Antoine Leroux, one of the best known mountaineers alive, came up from Taos with some companions to guide us through the Sierra San Juan into the Green River

region as far as the so-called "Spanish Trail."[28] After taking
leave of the hospitable officers at the fort, we started out to
execute one of our chief tasks, the exploration of the Coochetopa Pass. For four days we moved up the San Luis Valley
along the base of the Sierra Blanca in a northwesterly direction through fields thick with artemisia, the only thing which
grows well in the deep sandy soil. Sometimes we could see
fields of beautiful prairie grass toward the river and the river
banks covered with trees, but our experienced guide warned
us of the marshes, and we had to be satisfied with only the
view. According to his statement, the valley is very fertile at
the point where the Rio del Norte emerges from a cañon of
the Sierra San Juan into the plain. It has wonderful pastures
and is rich in game and wild horses.

The slopes of the Sierra Blanca are covered with cedars
and pines, but they are of pigmy size and suitable only for
firewood. Seen from this side the three- to four-thousand-foot
mountains of the Sierra display sharp ledges, although frequently they are more needle-shaped. At the foot of the
mountains lie numerous boulders, frequently of considerable
size, of quartz, granite, and a kind of basaltic rock. In the
mountains, as I discovered on an excursion in Roubideaux
Pass, these rocks have shattered and erupted through a rough,
bluish-violet mica slate so that all of the rocks together form
a real chaos.

Although no large animal population is to be expected in
this part of the valley, we still chased some grouse and sandhill cranes out of their hiding places and our hunters supplied
us richly with game. Competition for the game sometimes
appeared which proved as unpleasant as it was unexpected as

[28] Leroux also served as guide for part of the time on the Whipple expedition. See Möllhausen, *Diary*, II, 152 ff.

in the following incident. One of the hunters, who had come up from Taos with Leroux, shot a fat buck one day and was about to cross a little stream on his horse to retrieve it when a giant bear arose in front of him and gave him to understand that he had no further business there. The hunter had no other course according to the rule mentioned earlier than to turn his horse around and ride off, leaving the bear in undisputed possession of the buck.

Our camp on August 29th was almost at the northern end of the San Luis Valley on a creek containing many beaver dams, which held back the water and forced it to overflow, thus causing broad swamps to develop to the south. The ground over which we came was frequently covered by effloresced salts and only on the creek did pasturage and brushwood appear once more. The latter consisted primarily of two kinds of currant bushes, one with red and the other with black berries which had a pleasant bittersweet taste.

Fifteen miles farther north the valley is closed off by a low row of hills to form a beautiful park eight to nine miles wide and fifteen miles long. A number of streams, having their origin here and coalescing into a single creek, water the park, which is rich in luxuriant grazing areas. From here a convenient pass leads over an elevation of 8,600 feet, forming the watershed between the Arkansas and the Rio del Norte to the nearby South Park and the Sierra Mojada. The well-worn paths show that the Indians of the Río Grande and the Coochetopa region make frequent use of this pass. The Sierra Mojada or wet mountains, which get their name from the constant rainstorms there, extend from the northern part of the Sierra Blanca to which they are partially joined to the Arkansas. It is in no way to be regarded as a separate mountain system.

42

Peaks of the Sierra Blanca from near Fort Massachusetts.

Coo-che-to-pa Pass, view looking up Sawatch Creek, September 1.

A march of ten miles in a westward direction brought us to the entrance of Coochetopa[29] Pass. This entrance is marked by an isolated mound of bluish-gray porphyry which is situated like a guard at the gate. The way to the pass leads through the Sawatch Valley, one of the most beautiful valleys we saw on the entire journey. It is six or seven miles wide at the San Luis end but becomes narrow five miles farther west. The animals at first sink hoof-deep into the ground, which is light and powdery but becomes firmer and very fertile. Willows and cottonwoods thickly cover the banks of the Sawatch Creek, which waters the valley. The game in the underbrush is so thick that startled deer often leap across between our wagons. Grouse, too, are in abundant supply, and we catch beautiful trout, many weighing over two pounds, in the clear, pretty creek. The shape of the mountains, especially on the left bank of the creek, is unusually picturesque, mostly steep and eroded. These mountains offer the purest and most beautiful trap formations. A reddish porphyry with lustrous feldspar and mica provides the material from which these picturesque shapes are formed. The opposite side of the mountains representing the north side of the valley is less steep and covered with little firs down to the valley. Numerous herds of mountain sheep appeared frequently on the peaks of these mountains, protecting themselves from attack by a never-tiring alertness.

It is not more than about thirty English miles from the Sawatch Butte to the top of the Coochetopa Pass, but it took four days of the most intense labor to reach the top. Soon trees had to be felled to open a path for the wagons, and the mountain is covered with aspen right to the top; then a stream had to be bridged; and in addition the path led over sandstone and

[29] Coochetopa, gate in Utah language.—J. H. S.

43

wound around huge boulders of plutonic rock, which made it extremely tiring for the pack animals. About noon of the second of September, we reached the top of the pass as a light storm passed away as if to celebrate the event. Although we were 10,032 feet above sea level, according to the barometric level, the clouds still did not seem any closer than on the plain, and the little rain we received was unusually warm for this altitude. The astronomical observations showed 38° 12′ 34″ north latitude for the top of the pass, which lies on the great divide of the North American continent. The waters on the east side flow toward the Atlantic, those on the west side toward the Pacific Ocean.

From the top of the Coochetopa Pass we climbed down a gradual slope into the valley of Coochetopa Creek, which soon empties into the valley of the Grand River. The latter valley has a width here of a mile and a quarter, but it is compressed into a narrow gorge about eight miles farther west. The valley floor is even, covered with boulders, and apparently subject to annual floods. Grass grows abundantly here, and the banks of the river are clothed in willow bushes and cottonwoods. The mountains forming the upper part of the valley, which consist mostly of high, eroded layers of a white, fine-grained sandstone, have more or less the character of *mesas*, as the New Mexicans call level stretches of land ending on one or more sides in steep precipices. Grand River is a pretty, clear, cold mountain stream whose stony bed is a hundred feet wide and three feet deep. It is formed by the confluence of several branches, one rising in the northwest toward Leroux in the Elk Mountains, whose high masses lay before us in the West, the other rising to the north in the mountains lying west of the sources of the Arkansas. After following the east slope of the Elk Mountains, the Grand River turns south and west and

44

joins the Nahunkahrea or Blue River, which rises in the Middle Park and is incorrectly called the Grand River on all maps.[30]

We followed the valley of the Grand River almost two weeks, but we had to keep close to the slopes of the mountains for the most part, often at a considerable elevation, since the valley route was only rarely usable. This was a kind of travel in which great difficulties had to be overcome, of course. In effect, it was as though we had been engaged in a continuous crossing of the Alps since the middle of August but with the difference that some of the resources and comforts which a traveler in inhabited countries does not lack were more than a thousand miles away from us. The wagons had to be dragged up steep mountains and be let down the steeper slopes with ropes; rocky roads had to be cut through, ravines gone around, and strong mountain streams crossed; at times we had to follow a deep stream a quarter mile through the water before we found room to set foot on the bank and from there start to climb a steep mountain. During the whole time an unusual cheerfulness engendered by the pure mountain air reigned among the men and was expressed in loud, vigorous laughing. Even among the animals this air seems to have a similar invigorating effect. When the teams had to stop after heavy exertion in climbing the mountains to rest and catch their breath, they pulled afterwards with new strength without having to be driven. This pleasant, stimulating quality of pure mountain air is well known to hunters and trappers, and their conversation revolves about it as about a favorite subject.

The difference in temperature during twenty-four hours in these mountains is considerable but less uncomfortable than

[30] But the earlier names persisted with the result that the river which Gunnison thought to be the Grand is today called the Gunnison River after himself while the Blue River of the official report is the modern Grand River. George L. Albright, *Official Explorations for Pacific Railroads*, II, part 2, 101.

it would be in the flat land. While the thermometer frequently climbed to 25° C. in the afternoon hours, it had usually fallen to 2 to 4° before sunrise, and on repeated occasions in the morning we found a thick crust of ice on the water in the barrels. The weather was continuously favorable with the exception of a few days. The sky was usually clear with a light, pleasant southwest breeze or at worst only slightly cloudy. We had showers on only three occasions, during which the highest peaks of the mountains became covered with snow.

The farther one comes down into the valley of the Grand River from Coochetopa Creek, the more the sandstone found on the banks of the river recedes into the upper regions of the mountains. In the lower regions of the valley granite, gneiss, a rough silicious shale, and a fine mica slate are the dominant rocks. At the top of the mountains on the white sandstone and on those peculiar plateaus which form the *mesas* lies a violet-brown porphyry in horizontal layers fifty to a hundred feet thick. It consists of a base of compact feldspar with small crystals of glassy feldspar and mica. Although it resembles in appearance the porphyry found in the Sawatch Valley, it is more difficult to melt as seen in the reaction of thin splinters to the blowpipe.[31] The unusual extension of this rock and the peculiar circumstances of stratification make this porphyry an important and interesting object of investigation at a time when the question of the origin and formation of rocks has received new interest through chemistry. In its composition and entire lithological character, this rock, whose origin was believed to have been established with certainty as plutonic, apparently possesses the characteristic stratification of a sedimentary rock. For days it is encountered over great distances,

---

[31] This is exactly the opposite result from that described by Schiel in his official report. See *Reports of Explorations and Surveys*, II, part 2, 101.

and its horizontal stratification with layers sometimes pushed up vertically, but always of equal thickness, is seen on the highest mountain peaks without its ever going underground. Since it is more than probable, however, that this rock is of igneous origin, the discovery of the perhaps narrow canal through which the huge mass of rock flowed out of its oven to extraordinary distances must be of interest. A rock very similar to this porphyry appears in the Gray River Valley above the mouth of Cebolla Creek but it has become brown and blackish-gray through contact with the granite and very crumbled in the immediate vicinity of the granite. Colossal boulders of this rock, which goes underground here, lie upon the ground in the valley as if they had just climbed out of the ground. Their even surfaces, often worn mirror-smooth from sliding, show that this rock was at one time involved in a slow, sliding movement. If the identity of this rock with the porphyry could be shown with certainty, the solution of the problem of the origin of the latter would be very close. One often sees towerlike formations resembling ancient castles hanging over the steep slopes of the mountains, which give shape to the wild romantic valleys and cañons of the Elk Mountains and the southern Sierra de la Plata. They are the remains of a conglomerate lying under the sandstone and consisting of remnants of all sorts of plutonic rocks compressed into an extremely hard mass by a cement of carbonate of lime.

Although we knew that we were in the heart of the land of the Utahs, we had only once any sign of the presence of Indians. When we left our camp on September 8, the grass caught fire a short time afterward, and a thick smoke began to rise. Immediately a second smoke rose up some distance in front of us from one of the fires used by the Indians to telegraph the presence of strangers. This is actually the chief hunting ground of the Utahs during the summer, as many elk herds move here followed by packs of hunters. There is also abundant deer and antelope in these regions, the latter being hunted by the Utah Indians in a strange way, according to Leroux. They build the two sides of a triangle with boulders and shrubbery, and as they drive their game into the corner, the pack of hunters comes closer and closer together until they form the third side of the triangle from which there is no further escape. The wives have to assist in the hunt, and woe to the squaw who permits one bit of game to get through while the men are engaged in the slaughter. Inevitably she will be whipped.

There is no more beautiful sight to a hunter than an elk herd seen up close. Many a hunter would have envied me the sights I saw frequently when I left the wagon train with my assistants to make side-trips into the mountains. One day, instead of following the wagon train, which was forced to hold to the left bank of the Grand River along the top of the mountains, we went along the right bank of the river to undertake a geological reconnaissance, planning to meet our party about ten miles farther down the river. We were about to cross the river below a creek flowing into it whose ravine broadened into a beautiful pasture-ground near its mouth. Suddenly, through a wide opening in the bushes, our glance fell upon a herd of elk, forty or fifty in number, grazing quietly on the other bank. Surprised, we held still for a while to feast our eyes on the sight of these splendid animals and then tried to cross the river unnoticed. But the hoofbeat of our horses and the splashing of the water scared them off, and with their horns laid back they started up the steep walls of the nearby mountain with such agility that a few seconds sufficed to put them out of our sight.

The same day we came so unexpectedly upon the giant elk, we were surprised by a sight which promised us some real excitement. As serious as the situation might have been in this place and circumstance, it had a humorous outcome. We had ridden for several hours down the river on the slope of the mountain, picking up here and there a beautiful cornelian, a chalcedony of unusual shape, or a heliotrope, of which a great number lay strewn about on the ground, or else hammering a hyolite out of a rock cavity in the porphyry. Suddenly C[reutzfeldt] halted his mule with the cry "Indians," looking directly at an open spot about one and a half miles away on the bend of the river, undoubtedly the place where we were to join the caravan. If C. had seen correctly our position was extremely critical. Turning back was not to be thought of, for it would have taken a ride of some twenty miles by returning to the other side of the river and following the wagon tracks to catch up with our party. Furthermore, the wagons could have left only faint, uncertain tracks on the rocky, stone-strewn path which we could easily have missed in the approaching darkness. There was, therefore, nothing else to do but go forward with all possible caution. This we did but concealed ourselves as much as possible in ravines and behind elevations of the terrain. When we had come close enough to the spot to distinguish the objects clearly, we saw that what we had taken for Indian huts was a row of boulders which had strangely assumed the shape of wigwams. The supposed inhabitants of these wigwams consisted of some deer which had been grazing here and had run away as we approached. Soon the wagon train came down from the other side of the mountain, and after crossing the Grand River, camp was pitched. When I told Leroux how we had been deceived in such a humorous way, he recommended very em-

phatically that I discontinue all further excursions of this kind
if I wanted to keep my scalp a while yet. A few days later the
warning of this experienced mountaineer was shown to be well
founded. We had climbed down from a *mesa* to the bank of
Cebolla or Onion Creek and made camp when we were surrounded in just a few minutes by a host of Tabawatschi Indians, who seemed to have grown out of the ground in this
apparently uninhabited country. There were several hundred
men, women, and children. The men rode beautiful Navajo
horses for the most part, which they had undoubtedly stolen
from the Navajo Indians, who raise a good many horses and
sheep. Even some of the squaws were mounted and sat on
horseback just like men. They were for the most part well
clothed and did not have at all the famished, degenerate appearance of many of the prairie tribes. A certain prosperity
seemed to be the general rule among them. Their warriors
were powerfully built, of medium height with broad, high
chests but their legs had the usual bowlegged shape of all
Indian legs. Their faces maintained a very ugly expression
because of the great width of the base of their noses. The
speech which they addressed to us at first was overbearing,
almost threatening, and they made it very clear that if we did
not give them presents they would take them. With the intention of over-awing us with their strength and skill, some
of the warriors raced their horses madly back and forth, giving the riders a most demoniac appearance. Another means
calculated to intimidate us was their pointing to the surrounding mountains while continually chattering and shouting
"Utah! Utah!" According to Leroux, who fully understands
their language, they were informing us that two thousand
Utah warriors were waiting in the neighboring mountains.
Very recently they had had a great fight with the Comanches

and chased them over the mountains. The Utahs had never been defeated by any other Indian tribe. They lived in constant warfare with the Mormons and had killed many of them. They told us still more of the edifying details. But after Leroux had made a speech from our side, they changed their conduct. It sounded about as follows: "We have good weapons, much powder, and much lead. If you want to fight, so be it. We will fight with you and kill many of your warriors. The White Father has many brave warriors. He will punish your transgressions. He has sent us to ride through your land and to see what his red children are doing." The chief made a long speech in which he assured us that the Utahs had always been the best friends of the Americans. He commended us urgently to ask the White Father, when we returned to him, to send yearly presents to the Utahs, too, as he did the other tribes through whose lands his white children go. This was promised him, of course. Peace was concluded, the pipe was smoked, and the next morning the chiefs were summoned to receive some presents. These consisted as usual of woolen blankets, ordinary knives, brass bracelets, strings of pearls, small mirrors, red paint, and other trifles which delight the Indian heart.

The camp on Cebolla Creek was at the foot of a mountain ridge which reaches from the Elk Mountains obliquely through the Grand River Valley to the Sierra de la Plata, thus connecting the two ranges with each other. The astronomical observations gave the position as 38° 23′ north latitude and close to 107.5° west longitude. The barometric reading showed an elevation of 7,026 feet above sea level. From here one can reach the top of the mountains in two hours by following an Indian path. There to the south through the ravine of Cebolla Creek is a beautiful view of the snow-cov-

ered Sierra de la Plata, whose sharp, pointed or angular peaks
jut into the sky like giant columns. At our feet to the west
flows the Uncompahgra, which rises in the Sierra de la Plata[32]
and flows in a northwestern direction through a rather broad
valley to empty into the Grand River. Above the western
upland tower distant mountains, and Leroux named two of
the high peaks as Salt Peak and Abajo Peak. The former lies
on the so-called Spanish Trail leading from California to Al-
biquiu in New Mexico and is a favorite gathering place for
the Utah and Navajo Indians, who come there to trade. The
latter lies in the vicinity of the junction of the Green and
Grand rivers below the fords for the trail, hence the name
Abajo Peak.[33] On the east side are the neighboring mountains
about the Coochetopa Pass, and one can almost follow the
entire route traversed from the pass. North of the Grand
River, whose course is visible, the Elk Mountains stretch to
the north and northwest, and their summits seem to form here
a high plain cut off vertically on the western side.

The passage from Cebolla Creek over the fourteen-hun-
dred-foot mountain ridges to the valley of the Uncompahgra
was attended with great difficulties and took a full two days.
We had to make our path part-way through cactus and thick
fields of artemisia, part-way through thick oak bushes, with
long detours to avoid the deep, rocky ravines. The valley of
the Uncompahgra is several miles wide with light argillaceous
soil and completely without vegetation. Here and there effloresced salts are noticeable. Grass can be found only in places
along the river banks, which are also covered with willows,
cottonwoods, and buffalo-berry bushes. We had to cross the

---

[32] The Sierra de la Plata lies west of the Sawatch Mountains, the latter
being the Indian name for Sierra San Juan.—J. H. S.

[33] *Abajo*, Spanish for below or under.

river, thirty feet across and one foot deep, before we found enough pasturage for our exhausted animals. In the vicinity were some Indian huts whose inhabitants had fled with the exception of two old squaws. These two old women were very wrinkled and shriveled, with bleary eyes, and may well have lived through nearly a century. After the fashion of their people they wore their hair, which was still abundant and only slightly gray, cut short across the forehead and all the way around so that the back stood out bushily, giving them a hideous appearance.

After the runaways had convinced themselves that the two old ones had met no harm, they gradually came back and bore witness to their joy at their rescue from what they believed was certain death by jumping, dancing, and singing. One of the squaws who visited our camp brought along a large number of her descendants with her on the horse. One papoose sat in front of her, one she carried on her back in a kind of basket, and two sat behind her so that the horse was fully occupied from neck to tail. The clothing of these Indians consists of dressed animal-skins. Woolen blankets seem to be a rarity among them. On the next day, September 16, we met several small bands of men who all followed us to our camp, which we put up eighteen miles farther down the river, only a few miles from its mouth. They continued to arrive until late in the night, and their yells and calls to their comrades, asking where best to cross the river, were answered just as loudly by their comrades in the camp. There may have been two hundred warriors assembled in and around the camp when suddenly the war whoop was heard from several sides. This was either in sport or with the intention of testing our courage. They had recognized our guide, who had once shot one of their chiefs as the latter was trying to rob him of his horses.

Leroux showed not the least fear though he expressed regret that we might suffer some provocations from the red men because of him. He shared his night's lodging with the chiefs, who remained all night with him. The security officer informed the chiefs that if the war cry was heard again from any side, they would be fired upon. Most of the uninvited guests were sent out of the camp, but they made their fires close by and were now quiet neighbors. The watch was tripled that night, and orders were given to hold ourselves in readiness. We laid our weapons at our sides. Everything turned out all right, however, and most of our guests, who had not escaped noticing our alertness, left us at daybreak.

The principal chief of the band, Sireechiwap, had arrived during the night with his son, who actually held command because of the great age of his father. In the morning he repaired to the tent of the white leaders to speak and smoke. When Captain Gunnison through Leroux had explained the purpose of our coming, he answered: "This is your land and you can pass through it at any time. Across the mountains are bad Indians who kill white men, but the Utahs are good and glad to see the Americans." Presents were then distributed, pipes smoked, and some of the chiefs accompanied us for a distance.

The valley of the Uncompahgra just before emptying into the valley of the Grand River is several miles wide and the color of the river has become green. This color derives from a moss covering the stones in the river bed. It is not found in the upper part of the river, and the water there is clear and colorless. Leaving the valley for good, we crossed the Grand River some miles below the mouth of the Uncompahgra. We camped on the right bank of the river on a little creek which comes out of the west end of the Elk Mountains and empties after a short course into the river. The Indians call it Kahnah Creek. The next day after a march of twelve miles over loose, infertile ground we reached the banks of the Nahunkahrea[34] or Blue River. This stream enters the valley of the Grand River here from a magnificent ravine dividing the Elk Mountains from the western Roan Mountains. The Blue River is probably three hundred feet wide here, and its bed is for the most part deep. The current is strong, and the crossing with the wagons threatened to be an insurmountable obstacle. However, after some Indians had showed us a place where the water was not much more than two feet deep, the banks were cut down with axes and spades and the wagons were all brought safely to the right side of the river after more than three hours of great exertion.

The appearance of the Roan Mountains, which we had to our right for more than a week as we followed the course of the Grand River, is very picturesque. The steep slopes of the mountains are covered with a crumbling green sandstone and a red slate giving them an unusually bright coloring whose charm is nevertheless lessened by the desolate barrenness of the entire region and the complete absence of all vegetation. From the day we climbed down into the valley of the Uncompahgra to the hour we pitched our tents at the foot of the Wasatch Mountains about the middle of October, every agreeable characteristic of the landscape had disappeared with the exception of the view toward these mountains. The route led chiefly over argillaceous soil, sand or sandstone, which comprises several of the smaller mountain chains between the Rocky Mountains and the Wasatch Mountains. The western

[34] Schiel has misspelled the names of both streams mentioned in this paragraph, calling them Kaknah and Naunkara, respectively. Schiel had a great deal of trouble with Indian names and rarely does his spelling accord with that of the official report, which he apparently used as a reference. Corrections in the text are made hereafter without comment.

slopes of the Elk and the Roan mountains are made up of sandstone of all shades of color, a sandy, calcareous clay slate, argillaceous limestones of green and red, a sandy shale, and uppermost a soft, foliating, blackish shale which includes a good deal of fibrous and lamellar gypsum. From there washes down the dry, infertile soil of the lowlands along the Grand and Green rivers.

In the whole region there are only intimations of sedimentary rock containing organic remains. It almost seems as if there were as little organic life in the seas in which the layers of this deserted land were deposited as is to be found here at present. Only once did I find fragments of a dark gray limestone with numerous casts of shells, mostly amonites, together with a great many gryphaea strewn over the ground on the top of a sandstone hill. This was in the vicinity of Grand River where it turns southwest almost exactly on the 39th parallel some twenty miles below the mouth of the Blue River. I did not succeed in finding the rock *in situ*. A close comparison showed that these gryphaea belong to a species found by Pitcher in the cretaceous of North America and named *Gryphaea pitcherii* after him. Not far from the Nahunkahrea is a conglomerate of silica baked so hard that it has attained the hardness of granite, also a hard bluish limestone and a silicious slate containing much agate. But these rocks do not extend very far even though they were the only sedimentary deposits besides limestone which I could find in the lowlands.

It appears doubtful to me that the Jurassic system really exists in this region as claimed by a French naturalist, Mr. Marcou, and represented on his geological map of North America in Petermann's Journal.[35] If so, it must be in such

[35] August Petermann (1822–1878), German geographer and cartographer, was editor of a monthly journal devoted to geographical discovery and published at Gotha.

a rudimentary condition that it is very difficult to find, or it must have largely disappeared again.

It is a remarkable feature of the character of the whole country between the Rocky Mountains and the Sierra Nevada of California that whole formations disappear, as it were, before our eyes. The washing away of mountains takes place here on an immense scale and is the more easily observed as no vegetation of any account is present to hide the destruction from the eye. Nature seems here only to demolish without developing any compensatory creative activity. Several days before we found that tower-shaped conglomerate on the Grand River, we saw stones lying on our path which had no similarity to the surrounding rocks and which afterwards could be identified with the rocks contained in that conglomerate. As these rocks could not have been floated there upstream and to places lying a thousand feet higher than those towers, we must conclude that they are remains of a conglomerate that once spread that far and subsequently disappeared. On the slopes of the mountains in the Grand and Green River region as well as in the level valleys, the ground is strewn with a great many pieces of agate, cornelian, chalcedony, and other members of the quartz family, which could not be referred to any rock in the area. In the neighborhood of the Wasatch Mountains these minerals again make their appearance, but here they can be traced to a rock which still constitutes a large part of that range. The destruction may be followed there step by step. A similar and very striking washing-away process has taken place in the Elk Mountains with the black shale containing gypsum and the strata below it. Before reaching the banks of the Green River, we traveled for days over a black, clayish, absolutely barren soil produced by the disintegration of the mountain masses and found remnants of those strata in many places, especially in the vicinity of Green River. Here they form isolated hills of curious shape and often considerable size. Many have almost the shape of great churches or houses with colossal chimneys towering nearby. Where the dirty black shapes stand close together, one thinks he sees the ruins of a city whose inhabitants are buried under their fallen adobe houses or else flown from the awful, desolate region.

From the elevation of the taller hills lying east of the Green River one can look for great distances over the barren, wasted land. As far as the distant Wasatch Range one sees only a series of open, parallel ravines and fantastically shaped sandstone ridges without a trace of vegetation. A light cover of gypsum gives the soil the appearance of fields of snow. Neither the bald peaks of the northern Roan Mountains, nor the snow-covered Salt Mountains in the east, nor the broken and towerlike masses in the south are designed to lessen the gloom of this view.

With the nature of the country it was not possible after crossing Green River to hold to a strict western course, and we had to make a great detour to the north in order to avoid the impassable gorges, ravines, and obstacles of all kinds. After eight days we made camp on the San Rafael, which according to astronomical determination lay on the same parallel as the camp at Green River and not more than twenty miles distant from it. During this time we had more than one occasion to lament the absence of our guide. Leroux had left us at Grand River to attend to other engagements, leaving us to our own devices. Leroux and his companions had to make the return trip to New Mexico by night, staying under cover during the day, for if they had fallen into the hands of the

View of ordinary lateral ravines from camp, September 8.

Head of first cañon of Grand River below mouth of Coo-che-to-pa Creek, September 7.

Utahs, they would most certainly have lost their scalps. It took the experience, intrepidity, and cold blood of a man who had spent nearly fifty years in the mountains to deceive the sharp eyes of his deadly enemies and bring such a bold undertaking to a happy conclusion.

Before leaving us Leroux had described exactly the place where we came to the Spanish Trail and by following it could cross the Green River. Finding the fording place, which lies at 38° 75.5′ north latitude [*sic*], was made easier by a number of Akanaquint or Green River Utahs who crossed the river with their horses to wait upon us as we reached its bank. The Green River is probably 800 to 900 feet across here and has the same dirty red color which it has as the Colorado farther down. Its current is strong and its depth between two and a half and three feet.

The Little Mountain, sometimes called the Book Mountain because of its regular appearance, is several miles from the camp we erected on the right bank of the river. This mountain seems to be a continuation of the Roan Mountains and unites the latter with the Wasatch Range. Its steep slope shows horizontal strata several hundred feet high above which tower individual high peaks and ridges. Deep gorges and ravines cut into the mountain and give it the appearance of colossal, half-ruined fortifications. Desolate as the country is, this view is not without interest. Considering the fantastic formations on the other side of the river, the churches, temples, houses, and towers, one cannot escape the feeling that some wild, malicious tribes have dwelled here and destroyed each other in a furious war of extermination. In truth the Indian country is a land of wars of extermination.

The Indians who flocked to our camp seemed to be a

cheerful people. They laughed and chattered incessantly, and the trinkets given them brought them great happiness. A piece of bread with some bacon made them dance with joy.

Even though the number of Indians encountered between the Blue River and the Wasatch Mountains was small and the population of this region must be thin, it is still difficult to understand how these people can find sustenance in such an absolutely barren land. Subsistence through hunting is not possible here, for one can travel for weeks without seeing more than a pair of lonely crows or more game than a few contented lizards which seem pre-eminently to represent the animal life here. It is a region where, according to the saying of Kit Carson,[36] the well-known mountaineer, "not a wolf could make a living." Even the bulbous plants, which are an important means of prolonging a miserable existence for the tribes on the other side of the Wasatch Mountains, do not appear here. Only the buffalo-berries, found here and there on the banks of the larger rivers, provide a vegetable nourishment suitable for human beings. The soil is so poor and dry that even the artemisia and cactus fields, still a real annoyance to the traveler in the Grand River region, soon disappear, and only an occasional example of these plants reminds us of their existence. Only in the highest regions is the vegetation somewhat better, for here the frequent rainstorms, which reach the lowlands but rarely in the summer months, maintain the necessary degree of moisture. Here there is frequent opportunity to watch a cloud grow and swell very swiftly. But hardly has the mass attained some size before it begins to encircle the higher peaks or ridges, which alone receive the life-giving as well as the destructive effects of water.

The daily variations in temperature are very considerable

[36] Schiel identifies him as *Kid* Carson.

in this region, particularly in the month of September, when the thermometer frequently climbs to 33° C. in the afternoon and drops below the freezing point at night. Still, the climate is healthy and the expedition enjoyed the best of health as long as we were there. The appearance of the cochineal insect in these temperatures was interesting. We found an abundance of them in October in a small field of cactus on the San Rafael River.

Chapter II

*The Great Basin*

THE NAME Great Basin has been given to that strange land roughly between the 38th and 39th parallels, stretching from the Wasatch Mountains to the Sierra Nevada of California and taking in by far the greater part of the area of Utah Territory. Its elevation above sea level is not less than 4,300 feet, yet despite this high altitude, the area possesses a unique hydrographic system. None of its rivers, large or small, and none of its streams drain toward the ocean. They run off in the soil or empty into a number of lakes, many of them so shallow that they are hardly more than large swamps. Some dry up so completely in the summer, such as the lake lying on the east side of the Sierra Nevada and designated as Mud Lake on the map, that one can ride dryshod over their beds. They can even be crossed with heavily laden wagons, although only by the great exertion of the pack animals in many places. Only one of these lakes, the Great Salt Lake,[1] reaches any considerable size. It is more than seventy miles long and some thirty miles wide. Some of the lakes can be compared in size with the larger Swiss lakes, such as Pyramid Lake, the lovely

[1] The belief cherished by many that this lake once drained into the ocean is not justified by the topographical and geological conditions of the land.—J. H. S.

63

Utah Lake full of excellent trout, and Sevier Lake. The numerous mountain chains which cross the land usually in a north-south direction are never very long, but they frequently rise to more than eight thousand feet above sea level. They are sometimes connected with one another by spurs sent out by one of the ranges and designated as separate mountain chains in the popular topography of the region. They thus form long, closed valleys which sometimes narrow to ravines and sometimes have a considerable breadth with mountains or mountain-groups, chiefly of trachyte, scattered islandlike in their midst. While the view in a north-south direction is therefore very extensive, it is more or less interrupted from east to west by these mountains. But no matter how different the valleys in extent in this strange land, they have in common the same desertlike barrenness. The great sandy plain reaching far to the south from the central valley of the basin, not far from the west side of the Great Salt Lake, has no vegetation other than the unsightly artemisia bush, *Salicornia,*[2] at most some miserable willow bushes, poor grass, and some reeds or rushes directly on the banks of the Sevier River. The latter winds through this desert in the last part of its course after forcing its way through the Wasatch and Unkukooap mountains. In the upper regions of these short mountain chains crippled cedars and oak bushes may be found.

Even though highly picturesque landscapes are not uncommon in the basin scarcely a one possesses that friendly aspect lent by a fresh, vigorous vegetation. A certain gloominess is common to all of them. The view over the salt desert from the top of the Cedar Mountains, one of those small mountain chains southwest of the Great Salt Lake, is not eas-

[2] *Salicornia* is an annual herbaceous plant which grows on the border of alkaline lakes.

ily forgotten. The salt desert stretches forty miles westward from these mountains to the Goshoot Mountains[3] and farther north has a width of not less than seventy miles. I climbed a high peak while our wagons wearily sought to reach the top of a pass where they were let down the western side by ropes and cables. This was a procedure repeated frequently during our year and a half's wandering in the wilderness. From the peak I looked over a broad landscape surpassing anything I had seen in emptiness and gloominess. Crusts of a dirty whitish clay rose through the sand, which is covered for long distances with white salt crusts. As far as the eye could see, no trace of vegetation, no plant, not a blade of grass, not even the almost always present artemisia, no trace of any animal, no impression from the foot of a living creature in this bare flat ground. Naked, isolated clusters of rock rising here and there out of the ground to heights of almost two thousand feet threw dark, motionless shadows over the plain. The shadows of little clouds passing over the morning sun were the only living, moving things in that landscape, and they only heightened the gloom. If the eyes of a man from ancient Greece had beheld this view, he would surely have moved the entrance to his underworld here. We undertook the two-day march across this desert the following spring with a few Goshoot Indians as guides and were favored, at least the first day, by a bright sky from which all clouds disappeared in the course of the early morning hours. The trip was not without considerable interest for mirages filled the landscape with the most marvelous images. Since we knew the character of the land we could take delight in this sleight-of-hand without allowing

---

[3] These are the present Goshute Mountains of eastern Nevada. Schiel has here misspelled the contemporary term as Gashoos; elsewhere he has it correctly as Goshoot.

ourselves to be deceived by the bright and often wonderfully splendid images. I rode several miles out in front of the train with the astronomer of our expedition. The desert before us and to the south seemed bounded by an ocean with wonderful green islands, and once by chance we turned around and saw our long wagon train several thousand feet high in the air. The drivers were driving the animals with a whip, the animals were making heavy exertions, and the men were grasping the spokes of the wheel exactly as they were used to do in difficult places. We watched the heavenly driving, speechless with astonishment for half an hour; then the image faded and disappeared. A half hour later the train turned around one of the mountains which we had just pictured and which had concealed the train from our view.

The river valleys of the basin, of which only the Sevier, Humboldt, and Jordan deserve to be mentioned, share the desert features of the country with the exception of the last and the upper part of the Humboldt River Valley. Some smaller valleys pictured to us by the Mormons as very fertile, such as the Tuilla and the Cedar valleys, do not deserve this reputation. The Tuilla Valley ends right at the middle of the lake and is separated from the Jordan Valley by the Oquirrh Mountains. It is about twelve miles wide and twenty miles long and closed off to the south by a cross ridge with depressions, however, on both sides. The depressions on the eastern side connect the Tuilla Valley with the Cedar Valley, which discharges into Utah Lake. Only the eastern side of the Tuilla Valley possesses rather good soil; the middle and western parts are sandy and altogether infertile.

The water of all rivers in the basin is muddy and the riverbeds are never wide. Yet two of the rivers mentioned, the Humboldt and the Jordan, have a considerable depth and can be crossed only by boat or raft. Near Salt Lake City the Jordan has been bridged by the Mormons. The Sevier River offers fording places at many points as close as sixteen miles above the lake into which it flows during low water.

Toward the end of October we made camp on the Sevier sixteen miles above the lake, after descending the western slope of the Unkukooap Mountains. The weather began to turn cold and raw, and heavy snow flurries fell from time to time on the white sandy plain. The condition of our pack animals began to cause concern, and we had to think of moving into winter quarters as soon as possible to allow the exhausted animals time for rest and recovery. We therefore divided up into two sections to accelerate the work. The smaller section under Captain Gunnison's own command went toward the lake to locate it accurately geographically and place it on the map. The other section went upstream in a northwesterly direction to explore a ravine in the Unkukooap Mountains through which the river breaks in reaching the plain. According to the agreement, Captain Gunnison was to join us after about five days in the camp which we pitched on the west bank of the river.

The next day about noon a detail of soldiers was sent out from our camp to undertake a reconnaissance with respect to a convenient river crossing. They had hardly left the camp, however, when they encountered the corporal of the escort which Gunnison had taken along. Breathless, pale, swaying on his naked horse, he could tell us only in broken sentences after being brought into camp that the little band had been attacked at daybreak, as they sat at breakfast with no inkling of the impending danger, by a strong company of Utah Indians. He believed that all of them had been slaughtered with the exception of himself.

The rest of the military escort at our camp, not over twenty-two men, received the immediate order from their commanding officer, Captain Morris, to saddle up and hurry to the scene of the calamity thirty miles away and to salvage what could be salvaged of the situation. At the request of Captain Morris I had my horse saddled too and accompanied the little band on its very dangerous ride. After we had covered about fifteen miles at a fast gallop through the sandy desert, the strength of my horse, which was not very great, began to give out, and ten minutes later it fell over and lay lifeless. With a warning to watch out for some mounted Indians, who seemed to be spying out the region from the slope of a nearby group of mountains, I was left behind and was shortly thereafter alone with my dead horse in this barren wasteland. The party did not reach its destination until the evening was far gone. Men and officers remained the entire night with the bridles of their horses in one hand and their rifles in the other, awaiting an Indian attack which did not come. The soundless quiet of the desert was broken only occasionally by the howling of wolves or the cry of an owl. When the long, cold night was over they found the corpses of their murdered comrades, mutilated and partly devoured by wolves. It was a horrible sight.

After sitting for some time next to my dead horse and considering what could be done in this critical situation, I took my rifle on my shoulder, strapped on a revolver in a holster held by straps, stuffed my pockets with as much ammunition from my saddlebag as they would hold, and set out on the return trip to the camp fifteen miles away. When at nightfall I looked over the camp site from the elevation of a little sandhill, I found it empty. What had become of our people? On closer inspection of the site I found a horse with a lariat, grazing quietly in a corner of the terrain. I recognized it as one of the horses of the escort, and on further search of the bushes I found the rider, a half-dead Irishman, who in addition to the corporal had reached his horse during the attack and by hard riding had escaped the Indians. Closer exploration of the locality revealed that the wagon train had crossed the river probably to return to the camp site on the other side where we had camped three days before and which by agreement was to be the general assembly point. I succeeded in putting the thoroughly exhausted man on his feet, and after raising him to his horse, I guided the latter into the river. I then swung up behind the rider and drove the horse through the ice-filled Sevier. After a painful march we succeeded in finding the wagon train before daybreak. It had formed a so-called corral (barricade of wagons) at the foot of the mountains. After an extremely exhausting march of over thirty miles through deep sand, we arrived late at night at the camp site at the foot of the Unkukooap Mountains which was determined upon as the assembly point. Soon thereafter Captain Morris arrived with the escort. Several of his party had lost their horses and were still behind. A large signal fire was lighted to indicate the direction they must go to the stragglers, who were forced to hide from the Indians by day. Two days later we were all together again excepting those killed in the attack. Among the fallen besides Captain Gunnison and a number of soldiers[4] were R. Kern, the topographer of the expedition, and F. Creutzfeldt, my assistant[5] and likewise a

[4] Three privates were slain in addition to Gunnison, the botanist Creutzfeldt, the artist Kern, the guide William Potter, and a John Bellows for a total of eight. See Gibbs, "Gunnison Massacre," *Utah Historical Quarterly*, Vol. I., 67–75.

[5] There is nothing in the official report to indicate that Creutzfeldt was in any way Schiel's assistant. Creutzfeldt was official botanist, while Schiel was geologist and surgeon for the expedition.

German. These last two had accompanied Col. Frémont in the forties on his well-known exploratory trip into the Sierra Madre and had at that time barely escaped the fate which struck them so unexpectedly now. Still two more soldiers of the escort who had escaped death by a remarkable accident came back to us here. The one had found his horse in the attack and leaped on it, but the frightened animal threw him off again. He fell behind a willow bush, where the Indians left him for dead. The other jumped on a horse whose rider had just been shot down by the Indians and succeeded in escaping from the redskins, although they chased him fifteen miles.

Our most important topographical notes and some expensive instruments fell into the hands of the Indians during these tragic events, and if the loss of the latter could be endured, the loss of the papers meant a loss of a greater part of the work carried out over the last six months with the most strenuous effort in uncharted regions and often at great danger. It was, therefore, thought advisable to hurry as quickly as possible to Salt Lake City, 120 miles away, and through the intercession of the Mormons, who had only a short time before concluded a treaty of perpetual peace with the tribe, get possession of these papers again. At the same time we could get accurate information about the attitude of the remaining tribes before continuing our explorations. In any case the condition of our pack animals was such that the move to winter quarters could be postponed no longer.

Until the end of 1854 the understanding between the central government in Washington and the ruler of the Mormon state was a full-fledged *entente cordiale*. The central government had no lawful reason, nor did it seem wise, to mix in the foolish business on the Salt Lake, so President Pierce had once more named Brigham Young, the seer and prophet, to the governorship of Utah Territory after the expiration of his legal term. The annual income of a salary of several thousand dollars was not to be despised by a man with some thirty wives and a consequently large family. As long as this relationship, which only increased his authority among the believers, could be preserved, there was no reason for him to allow his loyalty to the United States to appear doubtful, and the Governor of Utah did not hesitate to protect the interests of the central government. An interpreter was immediately sent with presents to the scene of the calamity and, largely through the efforts of the president of the little community of Fillmore,[6] succeeded in recovering the lost objects with the exception of some of the smaller instruments.

The incident just described is more directly related to the outbreak of the Mormon troubles than may appear at first glance. The central government sent several companies of mounted riflemen under the command of Colonel Steptoe into these remote regions to punish the murderers of our comrades and make them understand that no distance would protect them from its strong arm. They forced the tribe concerned to deliver the instigators of the bloody deed. These were three warriors of the Pah-Utahs, and they were sentenced to three-year prison terms by a jury in Salt Lake City but escaped from prison on the third day and disappeared into the mountains.[7]

[6] The reference here is to Anson Call, a Mormon bishop and head of the Fillmore community, who volunteered his aid to Captain Morris in furnishing particulars of the disaster and recovering the scientific papers and equipment. See *Reports of Explorations and Surveys,* II, part 1, 75.

[7] Bancroft writes that "Orders had been given to Colonel Steptoe to arrest and bring to trial the perpetrators of the Gunnison massacre, and after much expense and the exercise of great tact and judgment, most of them were secured and indicted for murder. Eight of the offenders, including a chief named Kanosh, were put on trial at Nephi City; and though the judge distinctly charged the jury that they must find the prisoners guilty or not guilty of murder, a verdict of

The troops under Steptoe, however, were quartered in Salt Lake City during the coming winter, and from this time on the peace between saints and gentiles[8] began to break down. Among many women and girls of the New Jerusalem doubts as to the truth of the peculiar theory of salvation of Mormonism had for a long time been growing strong, too strong to resist a uniform which is so dangerous for the fair sex at any time. Their half, or third, or even less satisfied hearts responded willingly to dangerous temptation. Amorous adventures took place, followed by bloody clashes in the streets of the capital between the soldiers and the Mormon youth. It is well known how the long-suppressed resentment of the Mormons, nourished and intensified though not caused by these incidents, finally erupted in open rebellion against the government of the United States; how they refused to recognize officials of that government, allowed them to be mistreated by mobs and finally forced them to leave the territory; and how after driving out all the heathen, they took possession of the important warehouse belonging to the heathen merchants, Livingston and Kinkaid, "without paying for it," as the western papers say.

The journey from Fillmore to Salt Lake City leads through the more important Mormon settlements and the most productive part of Utah Territory generally. This consists of a narrow strip of alluvial soil which runs on the western side of the Wasatch Mountains, reaching a width of a

manslaughter was returned against three of the accused, the rest being acquitted. The sentence was three years imprisonment in the Utah penitentiary, this being the severest punishment prescribed by statute; but after a brief imprisonment, the culprits made their escape, or, as some declare, were allowed to escape." Bancroft, *History of Utah*, 493–94.

[8] The Mormons call all those who do not acknowledge their teaching gentiles.—J. H. S.

mile or more only in the Jordan Valley and in the vicinity of
Utah Lake. Farther to the south the soil becomes worse and
worse, and there are no streams like those sent down by the
Wasatch Mountains and used by the Mormons for artificial
irrigation of the land.

The main mass of the Wasatch Mountains consists in the
northern part of granite, gneiss, various conglomerates, and
sandstone. In the south trachyte, porphyry, slate, and various
limestones predominate, some of the latter of great purity and
dazzling white color, others richly infiltrated with agate.
Other mineral treasures are also found in the southern part of
the mountains: iron ore, sulphur, and coal have been found in
the vicinity of the little Salt Lake. I found whole mountains
of crystallized gypsum imbedded in a red and green marl in
the valley of Ungottahbikin Creek, a stream flowing into the
Sevier River almost at the 38th parallel. In the immediate
vicinity of Salt Lake City and in the valley of the Timpanogos
(Provo), carboniferous limestone with its characteristic fossils
is found but not coal, and the saints who inhabit this part of
the Territory have been exclusively dependent until now on
the Wasatch Mountains for needed fuel and firewood. This
mountain range is quite heavily wooded with firs, cedars, and
cottonwoods, but the trees reach no significant height, partly
due to the high elevation, partly to the long, hard winters.
The trees look like dwarfs in comparison to the magnificent
*pinus* of the Sierra Nevada, which grows at the same elevation
and latitude. The average elevation of these mountains can
be put at eight thousand feet above sea level, but some mountains, such as the permanently snow-covered Mount Nebo
near Utah Lake, reach a height of almost eleven thousand
feet. The Wasatch Pass, which goes over several mountains,
reaches an altitude of 7,820 feet above the gulf. This was told

us by Tewip Narrienta, an old Utah Indian and excellent guide, who attached himself to us in the vicinity of the San Rafael. There exists no half-way decent passage over these mountains between this pass, lying between the 38th and 39th parallels, and the so-called Emigrant's Pass, which leads directly to Salt Lake City. Through the latter pass goes the emigrant road from Fort Laramie by way of Fort Bridger. This road divides not far from the fort. Those emigrants who do not need to go to Salt Lake City to buy provisions or pack-animals and the like travel north around Bear River toward California or else take the Oregon Trail, which turns off at the northernmost bend of this river by way of Fort Hall.

The winters last a long time in the Wasatch Mountains. During a three-week excursion into these mountains during April, we found surprising masses of snow, and the thermometer occasionally fell to 14 or 15° below zero on the higher points. Ben Simon, a Delaware Indian, served us as guide during this tiring and adventurous tour, during which we lost several pack mules. Ben Simon had settled with his brother and squaws on the Weber River, while his tribe, certainly the most able of all Indian tribes, lives on the upper Missouri. We had many opportunities to admire his sense of direction and astounding memory for places. He described exactly to us regions where he had hunted eighteen years ago and had not entered since, and every time we found his descriptions confirmed when we came to the places described. How adventurous the life of such a mountaineer is can be inferred from the following episode from the life of Ben Simon. During a snowstorm on the high plateau near Fort Bridger, he told us about traveling with his squaw in this dangerous region some years before. It was midnight and so dark that he could not see the ground at his feet. The squaw sat behind him on

Summit of the nearest ridge south of Grand River traversed in passing around the lateral canyons, at noon, September 12.

View showing the formation of the cañon of Grand River near the mouth of Lake Fork with indications of the formidable side canyons.

the horse. Some distance away he heard a sound so low that only the ear of an Indian could hear and identify it as an arrow hitting weakly against a bow. He immediately held still and listened a while but heard nothing. He then climbed from his horse and laid his ear to the ground. Although he heard the same sound again, he knew that he had remained undiscovered for no Indian would make such a noise if he thought himself in the vicinity of an enemy or harbored even the faintest suspicion of it. He stood up swiftly and silently and held the mouth of his horse in Indian fashion so that it could not whimper, while his squaw bowed down on the horse's neck. Perhaps two hundred of his deadly enemies, the Shoshonees, who were on the warpath, passed by him so closely that judging from the sound he could almost touch them with his hand.

On top of the troubles of all kinds which await the winter traveler in the Wasatch Mountains there is an illness which will keep my memory of the sojourn in these mountains fresh for a long time. This affliction, well known to the Mormons, usually starts in the last months of winter or early in the spring. Its symptoms appear during bright, though not necessarily warm, weather after the victim has traveled over snow surfaces for several days with the consequent exposure to the reflected rays of the sun. There results a rather vivid, phlegmonic inflammation of the skin of the face, which is quite painful. Blisters form, giving the face the appearance of a large plaster having been laid upon it. The blisters are soon emptied, and the face is covered with a thick, disfiguring scab. To the great relief of the afflicted, this dries up in about two weeks and falls off, leaving behind a youthful epidermis. This tedious, even if not painful, process is frequently accompanied by an eye inflammation which is more painful than dangerous. Nearly half of our expedition was afflicted with eye inflammations, but everyone without exception had to go through the preceding change of skin to a greater or less degree. Even animals are afflicted with the eye inflammation, and the dog of our party, Delaware, a bulldog, suffered almost more than anyone.

The masses of snow in the mountains melt at the beginning of summer, and this with the fairly common storms and showers swells and extends the lake. But during the late summer and fall evaporation turns the balance, and the lake draws back leaving behind widespread sandcrusts on the higher parts of the shore and a white crystalline deposit on the bottom. Upon investigation of a piece of this deposit brought from a depth of ten feet, I found that it contained not less than 60 per cent sulphate of soda. I gave the Mormons the advice to build a furnace and convert the deposit to soda. They were very willing to do this if there had been anyone among them able to give guidance in the construction of a furnace and the manufacture of soda. But the skills of the chemical trade are not revealed but demand diligent and assiduous study, a disposition which is very inconvenient for the leading men of Utah, who assert that they possess all their knowledge through divine revelation. They must be satisfied as before to pay a florin and a half for a pound of ordinary soap, since they possess only the fats and not the soda necessary to its production. In those places where the lake has a considerable depth, this salt deposit must be very significant since at a depth of ten feet it was almost six inches. This concentration must become even stronger in the course of time because there are a number of hot sulphur springs around the lake which are responsible for an inexhaustible influx of salt. Such hot, usually sulphurous, springs are very frequent in the basin. Some forty of them break through the granite in an area of 150 feet at the eastern base of the Humboldt Mountains, forming one of the strangest and most interesting of phenomena.

Salt Lake City lies sixteen miles away from the Salt Lake at the western base of the Wasatch Mountains at 40° 45′ 30″ north latitude and at an elevation calculated at 4,350 feet above sea level from our six-months barometer readings (from November to May). The city is very amply laid out and visible from a great distance when approached from the south. Yet it does not make a very friendly impression, for though the streets are straight and wide, and almost every house has a little piece of enclosed land, everything bears the mark of poverty and makeshift. The streets, to be sure, have sidewalks, that is, by-ways separated by ditches from the street, but they are as impassable in bad weather as the streets themselves. In all parts of the city away from the central district, but especially in the southern part, pedestrians, riders, and drivers all have the same trouble in wading through the soft mud in the bad season.

The ditches mentioned above serve to conduct the fine water of a stream known as City Creek from the nearby mountains through the entire city, an arrangement which offers the inhabitants many conveniences. The houses are constructed chiefly of so-called adobe (air-dried brick), one-story high and covered with shingles. Log cabins are relatively scarce since wood must be brought a distance of thirty to forty miles from the Wasatch Mountains and consequently must be used sparingly. In the central part of the city there are some two-story houses as well as the new house of Brigham Young, the tithing office, and the statehouse, the latter the only house in Utah built entirely of stone. The tabernacle is also located here, a strange building constructed of adobe like all others in the city with a roof reaching almost to the ground. Since this house is to be used for church services only until the large temple is completed, the saints found it practical to adapt the underground space, normally used as a cellar or basement, for use as a kind of auditorium. The benches are arranged in amphitheatre fashion so that the speaker standing below can be seen and heard from all sides. As the ceiling of this hall is also the roof of the house and has the shape of a tunnel-vault, the height proved to be sufficient, and the two side-walls of the house needed to be no more than four or five feet above the ground.

The church service of the Mormons usually begins with a prayer of the high priest, followed by a song from the congregation which is accompanied by a good six-octave melodion in the absence of an organ. An Englishwoman, whose husband died on the way to California, is the organist and plays the instrument passably well. After the song comes a discourse by one of the directors chosen previously. The Mormons assert, of course, that the speaker learns only shortly beforehand that he is to speak, the speeches are made extempore, and anyone can be called upon to speak on a given subject. This is an excellent artifice to strengthen the people in the belief that revelations and divine inspiration occur continuously among the elect. After the service the tithing work is announced; every Mormon returns not only the tenth part of his labor but also the tenth part of his time. The congregation, however, is never given an accounting of the use of the tithe. When I remarked one day to the apostle Taylor, regarded as one of the most learned pillars of the church, that this was against the spirit of American institutions, he tried to explain to me that it was better in the end for the wiser and more learned to care for the affairs of a people than that the people themselves should bicker about everything. He pointed in all seriousness to China as his ideal of a form of government.

It is more irritating than amusing to observe how the poor, spiritually famished, generally very ordinary working people from Wales, Denmark, and Norway—these constitute the main population of the valley—are manipulated, fanaticized, and turned into pliant saints. It is not a new, but certainly an instructive, sight for the philosopher as for the statesman to see right under his eyes how a supposedly revealed religion arises and matures and how the crassest nonsense and most obvious deceit serve in the founding and establishment of a state for the purpose of exploiting the humble. Yet it cannot be said that the leading men of Utah are especially gifted or even talented. By far the greater part of them are indeed extremely ignorant and of limited understanding. Even religious fanaticism, which spreads like a contagion, is not found among them. They possess at most the fanaticism of selfishness, ambition, and leadership, which are common to shallow and deep minds alike, both inside and outside Utah. Even Brigham Young is no more than an unusual person. In a conversation of several hours which I had with him, I found neither knowledge nor unusual understanding on a variety of subjects. Yet he has great administrative talent, which is not exactly uncommon in America, a good measure of shrewdness, and he knows his flock well. A mythical teaching with high-sounding promises of worldly and eternal happiness has always captivated the ignorant, thoughtless man, and what must appear to the educated, thinking man as an unpardonable blasphemy is often welcomed by the great multitude and suited to its dim perceptions and way of thinking. There are many examples among the women of Utah of how the most foolish beliefs and religious fanaticism are able to repress or at least hold back the strong passions of mankind. In general the women in Utah are opposed to the doctrine of the plurality of wives, yet many are entirely resigned to it. I have even heard several of them express the wish that their husbands might take more wives, for "the more wives, the more salvation," as they expressed it. The wife can be saved only through her husband, according to the teaching of the Mormons, and it is therefore the duty of the man to save as many as possible. Psychologically, the most remarkable case of proselytization which I came across among the Mormons was that of an English family in which the wife and her two grown daughters went over to the Mormon religion, while the father remained unconverted but, because of a pliant disposition and the love of peace, came along to Utah. The women are sealed to the men by the prophet, an apostle, bishop, or patriarch—there is an unlimited number of these worthies in Utah—but although the relationship is legally called marriage and is considered such in practice, it is nothing else but concubinage so far as the ease of its dissolution and the position of the wife are concerned. If two men agree that they want to exchange one or another of their wives, they explain to the prophet or one of his representatives that they have had a revelation that they cannot save their wives but believe that the other one can. The other one has likewise had a revelation in which it was made known to him that he is the true savior. The sealing and unsealing has no further propriety than this.

Only the first wife has the position of a housewife in the Mormon household. Only she arranges everything and gives orders to the succeeding wives. While she bears the name of her husband, the other wives are called only by their first

names and, at most, "second, third wife, etc. of Brother N."
The lady elect always lives in the immediate vicinity of her
husband, but the others live crowded together in special rooms
or even in neighboring buildings, do the work of servants,
and occasionally see their husband. Many of the apostles even
have a number of wives in the neighboring communities and
visit them only now and then.

The saints boast that their religion is a cheerful one and
that a hypocritical gloominess such as found in Europe is impossible among them. The husband, they say, wants to see his
children properly happy and prosperous, and this is not the
worst side of their dogma. They love music and the dance;
their dances, where both old and young dance, are usually
introduced by prayer and song. Since spiritous drinks are not
on hand, there are no excesses at their festivities, at most only
too much dancing. Besides the dances, the theatre, naturally
an amateur theatre, is one of the chief pleasures of the saints
in the wintertime. I must say to their credit, although I admit
the dubious nature of this praise, that their theatrical person-
nel played as well and sometimes better than what is seen on
the stage of the larger cities of the West. The acting of a
Mrs. W., even in tragic roles, must be called excellent in view
of the conditions. They were not content with shorter plays
but played such things as *The Lady of Lyons* by Bulwer,
*Othello* by Shakespeare, *The Honeymoon*, and others. A favorite was *Jugomar the Barbarian,* the English version of
*Sohn der Wildniss.* The stage was narrow and the equipment
very scanty, but a great deal of effort was expended on cos-
tumes, which did not always correspond to the time and place
of the dramatic action. Thus the pseudo prince in *The Lady of
Lyons,* which takes place at the time of the French Revolu-
tion, appeared in the childish finery of a medieval dandy.

After the play there was usually another song, which was or became a comical song, in which the public in the pit (and the entire spectator space was all in the pit) sang the chorus, especially when the favorite Mormon Song was sung. In order to give the reader some concept of this *transwasatchian* poetry I will add a verse of this song in the original:

> *A Mormon father likes to see,*
> *His Mormon family agree,*
> *The prattling baby on his knee*
> *Cries: Daddy, I am a Mormon!*
> *Eh! the merry, oh! the merry, Eh! the merry Mormons*
> *I never knew what joy was before I came amongst the Mormons!*

The last two verses are repeated by the chorus. I regret that I cannot add the melody of this song for it fits the content completely. The theatre orchestra, which accompanies these songfests and is also active in the tabernacle, possesses a number of string and wind instruments. Although most of these are played incorrectly and often completely independent of one another, this does not stop the saints, completely unspoiled in a musical sense, from calling their music "the sweetest music on earth," an appellation whose harmless pride can well be pardoned. This "sweetest music" is like a large brewery which I was once told about in Salt Lake City. After finding the establishment in company of the topographer of our expedition, following a long search, I found in the corner of a kind of shed a brewing copper, which could hold approximately one hogshead, and a cooler that approached three feet in length and was no wider. The brew which came out of this apparatus was a bitterly sour travesty of the brewer's art. The descriptions of the Mormons concerning their own country are pure hyperbole and can be accorded little belief.

Even the descriptions of climatic conditions in their land are extraordinarily favorable and pleasant. If one would believe them, the climate of Utah is the most beautiful in the world. Sickness never occurs, and the few cases encountered are healed by faith, i.e. through the laying on of hands by the apostles. All of this is naturally the purest humbug. During our stay in Salt Lake City, an epidemic of scarlet-fever and measles raged, from which quite a number of children died. Several of the Mormons were bent upon buying the pharmaceutical materials which I could spare, and one of their apostles, whose wife had become ill, was so far from expecting healing by the laying on of hands that he did me the honor of asking me to visit the sickbed and give the orders.

The plural wives system of the Latter-day Saints has by no means been put into effect generally. Not every Mormon has more than one wife. By far the greater part of them are satisfied with one wife or must be satisfied because they lack the means of supporting more than one or because the most desirable women have been claimed by the dignitaries of the church. This situation combined with the insight of many into the shortcomings of an administration which could be thrust only on a herd of idiots and the agitation of the majority of women against the plural doctrine has led in recent years to divisions in the community and the multiplication of dissenting sects. This could have become dangerous to the authority of the prophet if he had not given the storm another direction by his rebellion against the central government, which brought the sending of United States troops and a response from the Mormons with their well-fed resentments. The plural system was apparently devised only for the advantage of the elect of the church which should cause no one to wonder. The prophet alone possesses the right to give permission for increasing the

83

number of wives to those whom he considers faithful, and this right he can assign to his delegates. The wife who marries outside the priesthood without permission marries hell. It may well be that the religious fanaticism so easily excited in many women makes paradise appear more certain in the train of an apostle or high priest than trusting their salvation to an ordinary saint whose own claims to a seat in heaven are less certain or even doubtful. These thoughts may be supported further by wifely ambition and vanity which survive under all fanaticisms. Those women whose less pleasing exterior would lead no man to the belief he could redeem them are also taken care of in Utah. Any woman can demand a man to redeem her "on the ground of the right and privilege of salvation" and the prophet who accepts her petition can order any man whom he believes capable of supporting her to "seal" her. Where not capable, he must present valid grounds for the refusal.

Their polygamous principles were held secret as long as the Mormons lived in the States. Only when they had emigrated to the Territory and believed themselves safe, did the associates and followers of the founder of the sect come forward openly with this doctrine. While perfectly suited to the inclinations of these gentlemen, it was supposed to represent an enticement for sensual unbelievers. The doctrine is based not only on the Bible but also on the New Testament, and they go so far as to assert that Christ himself had several wives. How close this theology is to the lunatic asylum is best revealed in a passage from the *Guardian*, written by the head of the apostles, Orson Hyde: "When in Christ himself the words of John are fulfilled: he will sow his seed and lengthen his days and the peace of the Lord shall prosper in his hands, then the Christian world cannot mistake its meaning. But how were they fulfilled? When Jesus was the bridegroom at the

84

marriage of Canaan in Galilee and took Mary, Martha, and the other Mary whom Jesus loved, this does not shock us. If a most proper affection and intimacy as between man and woman did not take place between our Redeemer and these women, then we do not know what is proper and what the marks of a good, decent companionship are. Discretion was wisely observed. But when the Savior, nailed to the cross, was breathing his last he saw his seed of children. Who will acknowledge his descendants? No one, if he had none to acknowledge. Despite the fact that this may appear to many a new and strange feature of Christian teaching, we are not inclined to scoff at it or to regret our salvation through the son of a virgin."

Mormonism believes in the Bible, but this belief is qualified by the assertion that the Bible, meaning the translation arranged by King James I and, of course, inspired—without inspiration or revelation nothing goes with them—is in the main correct but falsified by deliberate interpolations and errors. It was corrected and prepared again by Joseph the Seer to whom "the key to all languages" was given. According to the prophet-linguist, the Bible must begin as follows: "The Godhead begat the Gods." According to a later explanation this is supposed to mean: "The first God summoned forth the Gods and sat with them in a great council: the great council sat in the heavens and observed the worlds which were created at that time." God did not create himself (this was impossible), but intelligence existed throughout eternity as a spirit and had not been created. Smith's meaning about the origin of the Godhead is not set down in his writings, but the apostles have formed a kind of chemical-physical concept of it. We will learn more about it after we have given some space to some of the chief articles of the belief, taken from the

*Guardian,* in order to introduce at least some variety in this folly. These articles of belief read:

> We believe that the word of God is recorded in the Bible and also in the Book of Mormon and all good books.
>
> We believe all that God has revealed, all that he is presently revealing, and we believe that he will yet reveal many important things bearing on the kingdom of God and the second coming of the Messiah. We believe in the literal restoration of Israel, the re-establishment of the ten tribes, that Zion will be built on the western continent, that Christ will personally rule for a thousand years upon the earth, and that the earth will be rejuvenated and receive the glory of paradise.
>
> We believe literally in the resurrection of the body and that the remains of the dead will not live again until the thousand years are over.
>
> We claim the right to worship the almighty God according to our consciences and concede all men the same right.
>
> We believe that we are subject to kings, queens, presidents, rulers, and magistrates; that we should obey the law, and honor and preserve it.
>
> We believe that we should be honorable, truthful, chaste, moderate, charitable, virtuous, and upright, that we should do good to all men. We are able to say that we observe the admonition of the Apostle Paul, "We believe everything" and "We hope for everything," we have "borne much" and believe ourselves in a position "to bear anything." We look for that which is lovely, praiseworthy, and of good reputation and we wait for our reward. But an idler cannot be a good Christian, nor can he be saved; he is a drone and must be goaded to death or else thrown out of the body.

Since the content of the Bible must be taken very literally according to Mormon teaching, for God is candid when he speaks to men and does not use words ambiguously but "in their true sense," they come to a correspondingly literal conception of the essence and qualities of God. This conception is imparted in the sermons of the apostles and high priests, sometimes with a bit of humor. In a speech given by Brigham Young before the elders and high priests in the tabernacle, he said: "You remember the elder Day (a Baptist preacher on the way to California), who preached to us so handsomely. I preached one day when he was present and in the course of the address introduced some thoughts concerning our father in heaven, about whose nature he earnestly desired clarification. He ate with me at noon, and as we were sitting at the table, he said: 'Brother Young, I waited with anxious heart and with mouth, eyes, and ears open to hear something glorious.' 'Concerning what, Brother Day?' 'When you were describing God and had just come to the real point which I had wanted so much to have explained, you broke off and went on to something else.' I laughed and said: 'You are a preacher of the Gospel and have been preaching for twenty years about a God of whom you knew nothing? I can answer your question in a few minutes.' 'I know, Brother,' he said, 'it is a mysterious subject for a mortal man.' 'Now let me ask if you can tell me whom our father in heaven is like?' 'Brother Young, I do not flatter myself that I can describe the character of God.' He said this while the color of his face turned now pale and now red. I laughed and he believed that I was treating the subject lightly. 'I am not treating the subject lightly, but I am laughing at your foolishness, that you, a preacher in Israel, a man who is supposed to stand between the living and the dead, yet knows nothing of our Father and God. If I were in your place, I would never preach another sermon until I knew more about God. Do you believe in the Bible?' 'I do.' 'How did Father Adam resemble God when he was in Eden?' Before he could answer, I asked him further, 'How did Jesus resemble mankind when he became flesh?' and 'Do you believe Moses when he says God created man in his image, in the image of God created he him? This may seem strange to you, but do you not see that the Lord created Adam like himself and that the Redeemer, of whom we read, was the special image of his own person?' He now laughed himself at his own foolishness. 'Well, Brother Young,' he said, 'I had not thought of it all my life, and I was a preacher for twenty years.' He had never recognized the character of the God whom he worshipped but like the Athenians had erected an altar with the inscription: 'To the Unknown God.' "

The trinity is explained by Smith in the following way: God is the most perfect corporeal being, Christ is his son whom he begat of the Virgin Mary on the plains of Palestine, where the angel Gabriel proclaimed the marriage. The Holy Ghost is the concomitant will of Father and Son. The Holy Ghost differs from Father and Son in that he has only a spiritual existence and has never taken on a tabernacle, i.e. a material body, as the Gods have. Therefore, he did not die when he went through the time of temptation and resurrection to perfection. The origin of the Son is thus explained, but we want to question the apostles about the origin of God himself. We find that in remote eternity two pieces of elemental material came together in a consultation and compared their information with one another. They then summoned a third atom to the counsel and the three, merged into a single will, became the first power which no other could contain because it had priority. As it now joined more atoms or exercised the power which the union gave it, it set in motion the progress for all eternity. Out of this God arose, he was not created, and the other Gods sprang from him.

88

The talent for speaking in foreign tongues with no previous use of a grammar is one of the cherished privileges exercised in Utah. When someone feels impelled by the spirit, he stands on his feet, believing himself to be leaning on Christ, moves his lips, and brings forth a song in a favorite tempo, and the Lord will call forth an interpreter, and he will make a speech: so reads the precept. That these language exercises give rise to very humorous scenes, despite the efforts of the Holy Ghost on behalf of the one who is moved, is easily imagined. Think of a meeting in which someone suddenly rises and with all kinds of grimaces brings out something which sounds like: tschinah, puh-vah, kaka limasche! All is quiet, but after a short while another rises and explains that the Holy Ghost has disclosed to him what it meant, that it was some Indian dialect and meant—the translation follows. The most learned among the Mormons admit that the wag is not always missing on such occasions, for he will never die out in this world, and that Greek, Latin, German, French, and Spanish or any of the known modern or ancient languages are disdained by the Holy Ghost of the Mormons and never used.

I do not intend to go any further into the details of the different doctrines of Mormonism, such as the doctrine of the resurrection of the prophets and the priesthood, and the teachings about the sacraments, etc. My intention has been to do no more than describe the life of a sect about which relatively little is known in Europe, although its missionaries are secretly fishing everywhere, and to characterize a doctrine which has so far mislead thousands that they are ready to sacrifice their property and their lives for it.[9] One must not believe that their teachings are consistent even where they are compre-

[9] Just last summer a Mormon community was dissolved on Lake Zurich (Switzerland).—J. H. S.

hensible. On the contrary, for every tenet, every assertion, and every so-called revelation in the various works of the scribes, there is a contradictory tenet, assertion, or revelation. The entire system is a chaos of nonsense, contradiction, and monstrosities of all kinds but promulgated with that confidence and audacity which has impressed and captured the ignorant, unthinking man through all history.

As monstrous as Mormonism itself are the expectations of the saints for the future. Not only will the privileged man rejoice in the time about which Josiah prophesies "when seven wives will take hold of a man and say: we want to feed and clothe ourselves, only let us be called by your name that our shame may be taken from us," but the true church of God will spread over the earth and finally absorb all other sects. The new Jerusalem will be built in Jackson County in Missouri, and all of Christendom will divide into two great camps, the one under the banner of Rome, the other under the flag of all nations. A great battle will be fought in which the saints will win with the help of God, who will fight for them with fire, hunger, and pestilence. Then begins the thousand-year kingdom, but first the Jews will rebuild the temple of Solomon in Jerusalem. Their long yearned-for savior will come, descend on the pinnacle of the temple, and reveal himself to the people in his entire majesty. The earth, divided in Noah's time, will be reunited, and between the two Zions a road will be built "which the lion has not trodden and the eye of the eagle has not seen." It will be built with houses and villas in uninterrupted rows. After the thousand years the rebellious spirits will be given a short time to try their might, but they will be smitten down to the ground and banished, and the earth will appear from now on in its paradisiacal glory.

As a religious community the Latter-day Saints might

Rock Hills between Green and White rivers, October 3, Wasatch Mountains in the distance.

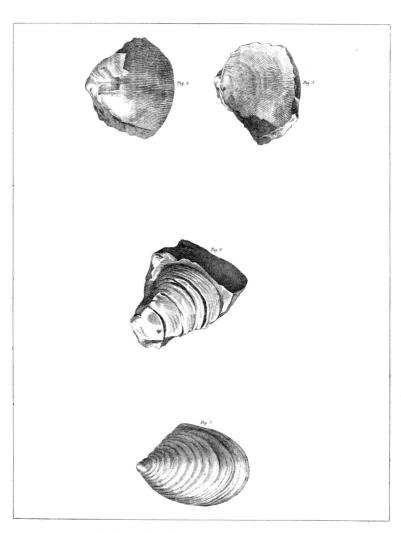

Geology plate 2, from sketches by Schiel.

have been able to ask for the free exercise of their religious views and would probably have been granted it on the free soil of America, but as a political body inhabiting a territory of the United States with institutions like theirs, it was inevitable that they should come into conflict very soon with the government of the United States. Their state is ruled by the seer and prophet in the name of the Lord, who makes His will known through him. This arrangement they called a theocratic democracy, and the people stand in relation to the prophet as the children of Israel once did to Moses. Two counsellors to the seer are appointed, and the three together constitute the executive; aside from these three, there are twelve apostles or elders in Israel, and the whole number makes up the higher priesthood of the order of Melchisedek. The second order is that of Aaron; it includes the lesser priests, the so-called quorum of seventy, deacons, bishops, teachers, etc. and some jurisdiction is likewise put in the hands of this lesser priesthood. The state has an elected legislature, but it can make no laws contrary to the will of the prophet. It can only apply the laws derived from the divine will to the social conditions of the people. That the divine will is never contrary to the interests of the high priesthood never troubles any good Mormon. If it should happen anyway, he has listened to the promptings of Satan. It is very clear that under such arrangements gentiles and Mormons cannot live side by side.

When one sees what the Mormons have made of their country since taking it over, he cannot withhold praise of their diligence and perseverance, but the great admiration which they have for themselves has not been earned. Compared with what has been accomplished in California in lesser time by the overland emigration, their accomplishment seems very small even when all of the differences are taken into account. The person who does not mistrust the descriptions of the Mormons as exaggerations and deliberate lies must come to the conclusion in reading them that the Jordan Valley is a paradise in which wonder crowds on wonder. In reading of wonderful national workshops where everyone can find employment until he can make himself independent, one has to think of some sheds with several workbenches, circular saws, vises, and lathes standing in them, all in rudimentary condition, with less than a dozen men working at them so far as I could see. The workshops appear to enjoy no great favor even among the saints themselves. It is similarly the case with their educational facilities. They exist only as an idea. The school system in Utah has not gone beyond the elementary level which is of course understandable and quite common. Even their great cotton manufacture is a chimera. In an attic room of the statehouse the Mormons keep several expensive scientific instruments which they offered to me for my use during the time of our stay in Salt Lake City, since they still had no one among them who knew how to use them. There was an excellent Ross microscope of the newest design, and the astonishment of some of their learned scribes at the real marvels which the little instrument revealed to them, when I showed them several objects, was very great. They had no fewer than six barometers for measuring elevation made by the well-known English inventor, Troughton, but all had gotten air in their vacuums or had been otherwise damaged by careless handling. Not a single one was usable. A chemical apparatus in the form of a large reagent box was also there, likewise a telescope and some smaller measuring instruments. A part of the library, for whose creation Congress had earlier granted five thousand dollars, recently went up in flames. In addition to the great English encyclopedias, the science of jurisprudence had been rather well represented, and it is asserted that the fire was started with the foreknowledge of the Mormon authorities to whom jurisprudence was especially unwelcome.

The description I have given of the land of Utah is not clothed in the rosy colors of the saints, but it is, I believe, a true picture of conditions which have aroused general interest on this side of the ocean and even more on the other side. It gives me special pleasure to be able to give assurance that in the entire Territory I met no more than three Germans who had entered the community of the Latter-day Saints and the faith of one of them, at least, was not built upon rock. The principal of these three worthies was a penniless student, who from necessity had translated the Book of Mormon into German and then followed the missionary for whom he had done this work from Hamburg to Utah. He was the city engineer in Provo, the second city in size, and was waiting impatiently for the Holy Ghost to reveal to him the theorem of congruent and analagous triangles, since without this knowledge his vocation was turning very sour. The second countryman was a barber, who hoped to trim the beards of all nations following their conversion, but in the meantime, complaining about the high price of shaving soap, he did some doctoring in the big city. The third was a very ordinary man. In making the acquaintance of the first of these three Germans, a coincidence was revealed which deserves to be told. One of the Mormon apostles (Apostle Taylor) asked me one day if he could introduce to me a young German who lived in Provo and was very anxious to see one of his countrymen. As I was agreeable, he brought the young man to me several days later. It was the translator of the Book of Mormon. During my conversation with him I mentioned by chance the fact that I had been in Russia in the year 1847. At this remark the young man got up

93

from his seat and said, "It just came to me that I have seen you before somewhere." He named the steamer on which I had arrived in Kronstadt, described a friend of mine exactly and a part of the company with which I made the trip, and the circumstances of our arrival. Finally, enjoying my astonishment, he added: "You had to go with your friend on a little ship in Kronstadt to have your passports inspected. Would you recognize the officer again who inspected them?" When I replied no, he said, "I was that officer." He now explained to me that he later went to Hungary with the army under Paskevich, that several divisions of the Russian army had gone over to the Hungarians there,[10] and that he was helped in escaping to Vienna and then to his home town, Hamburg, after Görgey had laid down his arms. How he came to the Mormons has already been explained above.

If I have done any injustice to the Latter-day Saints in the foregoing description, I would regret it the more since I must close with a great incivility to the women of Utah. I make this transgression in the interest of consoling those of my countrymen who may look with silent envy and perhaps secret desire upon the prerogatives of the saints. In the entire valley[11] I saw not a single beautiful woman, or even one approaching it, and only one girl who, while quite pretty, was not the type to "shake the saintship of an anchorite"; yet she can await salvation with certainty, for compassion still lives in Utah. May all the daughters of Utah forgive me that I have no better opinion of their charms.

On the sixth of May we left Salt Lake City to continue

---

[10] I am far from vouching for the truth of this part of his story.—J. H. S.

[11] "In the valley" means to live among Mormons. The expression applied originally to the Jordan Valley and was gradually extended to the whole Territory. There is no Utah Valley, of which one reads from time to time.—J. H. S.

our exploration of the country to the west.[12] Passing through the country between the southern shore of the Salt Lake and the northern end of the Oquirrh Mountains in five days, we climbed over the Cedar Mountains in order to cut through the salt desert lying west of these mountains. Sho-ish, a Utah chief, had sent a runner to his tribe, the Goshoot Indians, to say that we were his friends and had given beautiful presents to his brethren; this caused several of them to present themselves at our camp to serve as guides. We put them on mounts in order to make better progress.

The journey over the salt desert, whose character we described earlier, is practicable only in the dry season and takes two days. The first day brought us to the middle of the desert to the foot of a tall group of trachyte rocks, from which several clear springs of sweet water bubbled. No trace of grass for the animals was to be found and only after a painful march of more than twenty-five miles were the exhausted animals able to refresh themselves in the fresh pastures which we found at the foot of the Goshoot Mountains. The weather was less favorable the whole second day, but the clouds protected us from the reflection of the sun's rays from the effloresced salts covering the ground. This reflection of the sun's rays is very painful to the eyes, and even light clouds do not alleviate it entirely. The storm clouds which hung about the high peaks all day finally united in a severe thunderstorm toward evening. The rain was accompanied by a strong windstorm which sent heavy hailstones against us. During the storm our mules would not be driven forward. They turned around with their backs to the storm and would not stir until it had passed. During this hurricanelike storm a great many artemisia bushes

[12] The date in the official report is given as May 5. *Reports of Explorations and Surveys,* II, part 2, 20.

from the three-mile-wide artemisia field enclosing the salt desert on the west were uprooted and carried away.

Many beautiful springs arise in the syenite masses of the Goshoot Mountains and sometimes form little mountain streams which roar down into the plain and are responsible for some beautiful pasture-ground. Many of these streams contain little fish, and the Indians call them *pangwich* (fish waters). A great many of the most beautiful hornblende crystals were obtained with little effort from this rock, whose surface has been badly weathered everywhere.

Before we reached the foot of the mountains our guides, who seemed to be a most merry band of thieves, climbed off their horses to make their toilets in honor of their brethren, whom they were soon to meet. For this purpose they dug several inches into the earth where they found a white clay with which they smeared their faces over and over. We then received the visit of the expected guests, who were almost completely without clothing, dirty, and emaciated by starvation. In summer rats, lizards, and crickets serve as their nourishment, but in winter this game is lost to them or at least is very rare, and they are dependent for their subsistence upon some bulbous plants and the seeds of smaller plants, thus being reduced to the greatest extreme of want. We gave them something to eat and several small gifts which brought them unwonted pleasure.

The land from the Goshoot Mountains to the Humboldt Mountains was partly rolling, partly more broken up and hilly. The lower hills consist chiefly of the remains of an indurated clay which seems to have covered a wide area formerly but is mostly washed away at present; others consist of a soft, crumbling sandstone. The more prominent hills consist chiefly of granite and metamorphic rocks. The inevitable artemisia bushes and cedars flourish in abundance in the entire area.

We met a group of about twenty Shoshonee Indians with their wives and children west of the Goshoot Mountains. They were well provided with buffalo hides and blankets, although they complained a great deal of hunger. They instilled such a fear in our guides that they turned back immediately to their own people, although three of them appeared again later. About noon of the day we reached the base of the Humboldt Mountains, we saw smoke curling up in the neighborhood of a spring. It came from a Digger wickeyup (wigwam) or hut, which consisted of nothing else but a stunted cedar bush. The inhabitants of this nature-hut were a man and a rather young woman. The former ran off in fright when he saw us, but the squaw noticed us only after it was too late to run away, and she was caught by one of our party and brought into the camp. The man watched us from a distance, and after convincing himself that the squaw was suffering no harm, he appeared in our camp, although trembling violently in his whole body. He gave us to understand as well as he could that he had taken us for enemy Shoshonees. A more hideous picture of ugliness and dirt than this squaw cannot be imagined. Covered only by squirrel skins and dirt, discharges ran out of her mouth, nose, and eyes onto her body. In a little basket she carried artemisia seeds which she ground between two stones for food for two emaciated, mean-looking dogs which accompanied her. She was constantly beating the animals on the head with a thick club to keep them from lapping the mill-stones. A pot of meal-gruel was placed before the unclean pair, but they would not eat from it until one of our party had made them familiar with the use of the spoon. Some small gifts, knives and some pieces of cotton cloth, brought them no little astonishment. These Digger Indians are no special tribe but

97

consist of the refuse of neighboring tribes and make up a kind of criminal colony. Even their language seems to be a mixture of the dialects of the Indians living nearby. So far as intelligence and physical development are concerned, these people are certainly at the lowest level of the species.

On the 20th of May we reached the foot of the Humboldt Mountains, which lie about six thousand feet above sea level. Of all the mountain chains which cross the Great Basin between the Wasatch Mountains and the Sierra Nevada, this is by far the most important. The average height of the Humboldt Mountains can be taken as about eight thousand feet, although the mountain masses in the northern part of the chain reach a height of nine thousand to ten thousand feet. The blanket of snow lying on them at this season reaches several thousand feet down from the top of the mountains. The mass of the mountains consists chiefly of granite, which in the north passes into a dense quartz. The latter assumes in many places a shaly structure. Upon the granite to the south lies a dark limestone which resembles the carboniferous limestone from the vicinity of Salt Lake City but I was not successful in finding the corresponding fossil remains. The mountains send numerous mountain streams down into the plain, which spread to a width of several miles at the foot of the mountains to form a number of lakes or, more nearly, morasses of limited depth. In and around them a long, rush-like grass grows luxuriantly. The largest of these mountain streams, to which we gave the name Franklin River, flows in a northern direction, breaking through a narrow, almost ravinelike valley in the north of the mountains and coalescing with another main branch of the Humboldt River.

About one and a half miles from the middle of the mountains one can see a dense vapor in the far distance on the plain.

It comes from some forty hot springs which break through the granite in an area of at most 150 feet. The pipe-shaped canal of most of them is broadened into a funnel shape at the surface. In the pools which they form a slimy deposit of sulphur is noticeable. The temperature of the water is 56° C. It contains such a small quantity of sulphuric salts, chloride, and hydrothionic acid that after cooling it is completely tasteless.

Another phenomenon to delight the view in this by no means benevolent landscape is found right at the foot of the mountains not far from the hot springs. It is a huge spring eight to ten feet wide and several feet high which tumbles with a roar and great force out of the limestone mentioned into a deep ravine, where it forms a powerful stream which nevertheless runs off in the argillaceous sandy plain after a short course.

For the first time since we left Salt Lake City we saw some antelope, ducks, and sage chickens here, but we did not succeed in getting our hands on one of these animals. Usually only lizards are seen in this area, and the species seems to be represented as far as the Humboldt River by numerous, often very fine and magnificently colored specimens. The rattlesnake appears here also, although many travelers assert that it is not found west of the Rocky Mountains. I had opportunity to convince myself to the contrary. While our wagon train was laboriously working its way through a narrow ravine one day, I sat down before the entrance to the ravine on a block of stone, holding my horse's reins in my hand. Suddenly, I heard beneath me the familiar whirring, sinister rattle of a snake. I jumped up quickly and looked at the stone but found nothing and sat down again, taking the whole thing for an illusion. Immediately the same sound was heard again, and upon closer examination I now found that the block of stone

99

lay in a hollow position and a large rattlesnake was concealed underneath. I stepped a bit to the side and holding the barrel of my gun right in front of the hollow I fired at the animal. The snake was about five feet long and had thirteen rattles. I was not able to say whether it was a special species, because the head was shot up so badly that I left the animal as unfit for an examination or for the collection. Aside from those mentioned above, almost the only animals we encountered on our way from the Salt Lake to the Sierra Nevada were a few rodents, particularly the so-called ground squirrel or Norway rat, and some birds of prey, hawks and eagles.

Until the twenty-seventh of May we went in a southern direction along the base of the mountains almost precisely to the 40th parallel, where a depression in the mountains permitted an easy crossing. Here we met some better fed and clothed Digger Indians than we had been used to seeing, and soon others flocked around us. In their company there was only a single squaw, who had a one-year-old child with which she walked about very tenderly. We gave her some pieces of cotton cloth with which she dressed her child. It was for us an unusual sight not encountered on our entire journey to see the father of the papoose play tenderly with it. The entire company owned only one horse on which they had packed all of their belongings. The child sat on top, the father walked beside, and the squaw was not required to drag some burden, all of which was uncommon among the Indians.

Several days after crossing the Humboldt Mountains, we met some Indians who were busy catching ground squirrels. The animals are numerous and fat at this season. They are killed with blunt arrows, caught in traps which have almost the shape of the figure 4, or else dug out. Some had forty to fifty of them hanging from their sides, the harvest of a single day. About forty of the band, most of them unarmed, appeared toward evening in our camp. A few kettles of soup and some small presents, knives, beads, etc. brought them such joy and put them in such a good humor that they spent the whole night singing and making noise around the fire, thus making it impossible for us to sleep. Their song consists of a monotonous, grunting nasal sound "Hoheio, hoheio, hoheio," which sometimes falls a fourth, from where it is raised again to the preceding level. Sometimes they muffle their voices to the point of vanishing, only to break out again with a truly infernal noise. At daybreak their number grew to fifty, and the chief of the band also appeared with his small son to receive presents. They were both dressed in scarlet red blankets which made them not a little proud. The importuning of the other late arrivals was turned down with a "kay-wit."[13] Their wigwams, in their language wickiups, look better than those of their eastern brethren. They have the shape of a bee-hive, are four to five feet tall, usually covered with grass and twigs, and have an opening on the north side which serves as an entrance. The location of this entrance make the traveler aware that rain and storms always come from the south in this country.

The entire country between the Humboldt Mountains and the Sierra Nevada of California is a rugged mountain area with only the most miserable vegetation. Only here and there on the slope of a mountain or in the narrow valleys and ravines can one find grass for the animals. A tree is a rarity in these barren regions. The mountains are composed of quartz, trachyte, a dioritic rock, the dark limestone mentioned above, sandstone, and a limestone conglomerate which is encountered on the highest peaks of the mountains. The most remarkable

[13] Corresponds with the German "nichts mehr" (no more).—J. H. S.

rock met here is an agate or more accurately a conglomerate of agate, chalcedony, and jasper welded together by heat to a compact whole. West of the Humboldt River we find quartz, syenite, granite, and a clay slate, but the closer we come to the Sierra Nevada the more these recede and eventually give way completely to the younger igneous formations.

# ELEVATIONS AND GEOGRAPHICAL LOCATIONS

of some of the notable places between the Missouri and the Sierra Nevada of California. (The elevations are in relation to a sea level corresponding to a barometric level of 30″ and 0° mercurial temperature and a median air temperature of 14° C.*)

| Name of the Place | Elevation above Sea Level in English Feet | Location in North Latitude ° | ′ | ″ |
|---|---|---|---|---|
| Pawnee Fork | 990 | 38 | 11 | 03 |
| Fort Atkinson | 2,330 | — | — | — |
| Big Timber of the Arkansas | 3,328 | 38 | 13 | 18 |
| Bent's Fort | 3,671 | 38 | 03 | 27 |
| Apishpa | 4,723 | 37 | 56 | 42 |
| Huerfano at the Mouth of the Arkansas | 6,099 | 37 | 43 | 10 |
| Cuchara | 6,109 | 37 | 38 | 30 |
| Foot of the Spanish Peaks | 7,463 | 37 | 42 | 25 |
| Sangre de Cristo Pass | 9,396 | 37 | 36 | 52 |
| San Luis Valley | 8,365 | 37 | 30 | 26 |
| Entrance to the Sawatch Valley | 7,567 | 38 | 07 | 46 |
| Coochetopa Pass | 10,032 | 38 | 22 | 06 |
| Grand River | 7,293 | 38 | 29 | 02 |
| Uncompahgra River | 5,332 | 38 | 42 | 38 |
| Blue River (Nahunkahrea) | 4,410 | 39 | 07 | 24 |
| Green River | 3,828 | 38 | 57 | 26 |
| San Rafael River | 5,718 | 39 | 00 | 30 |
| Top of Wasatch Pass | 7,820 | 38 | 45 | 37 |
| San Pete Creek | 4,960 | 39 | 09 | 58 |
| Sevier River | 4,692 | 39 | 20 | 57 |
| Nephi (Mormon settlement) | 4,938 | 39 | 41 | 56 |
| Provo | 4,362 | — | — | — |
| Salt Lake City | 4,351 | 40 | 45 | 37 |

* This is the median temperature in the latitudes concerned.—J. H. S.

| Name of the Place | Elevation above Sea Level in English Feet | Location in North Latitude ° | ′ | ″ |
|---|---|---|---|---|
| Weber River in the Kamas Prairie | 6,319 | -- | -- | -- |
| Timpanogos in the Kamas Prairie | 6,242 | -- | -- | -- |
| Divide between Muddy Creek and Bear River | 8,133 | 41 | 15 | 43 |
| Franklin River, eastern foot of the Humboldt Mountains | 6,004 | 40 | 34 | 52 |
| Pass in the Humboldt Mountains | 6,848 | 40 | 19 | 00 |
| Humboldt River | 4,140 | 40 | 42 | 00 |
| Valley of Mud Lake | 4,134 | 40 | 41 | 48 |
| Foot of the Sierra Nevada | 4,118 | -- | -- | -- |

# Bibliography

Albright, George L. *Official Explorations for Pacific Railroads.* University of California Publications in History. Berkeley, 1921.

Bancroft, Hubert H. *History of Utah.* The History Company, San Francisco, 1890.

Billington, Ray A. *Westward Expansion.* The Macmillan Company, New York, 1949.

Creer, Leland H. "The Explorations of Gunnison and Beckwith in Colorado and Utah, 1853," *The Colorado Magazine,* VI, 184–92 (Sept. 1929).

———. *The Founding of an Empire.* Bookcraft, Salt Lake City, 1947.

Davis, Jefferson. *Report of the Secretary of War Communicating the Several Pacific Railroad Explorations.* 3 vols., Washington, 1855.

Gibbs, Josiah F. "Gunnison Massacre—1853," *Utah Historical Quarterly,* I, 67–75 (July, 1928).

Gunnison, John W. *The Mormons.* Lippincott, Grambo & Company, Philadelphia, 1852.

Kelly, William. *Across the Rocky Mountains from New York to California.* Simms and McIntyre, London, 1852.

Möllhausen, Baldwin. *Diary of a Journey from the Mississippi to the Coasts of the Pacific.* Translated by Mrs. Percy Sinnett. 2 vols. Longman, Brown, Green, Longmans and Roberts, London, 1858.

105

Olshausen, Theodor. *Geschichte der Mormonen.* Vandenhoeck and Ruprecht, Göttingen, 1856.

Park, William L. *Pioneer Pathways to the Pacific.* Clara Aire, Clare, Michigan, 1935.

Johann Christian Poggendorff. *Biographisch-literarisches Handwörterbuch zur Geschichte der exakten Wissenchaften.* 5 vols. J. A. Barth, Leipzig, 1898.

*Reports of Explorations and Surveys to Ascertain the Most Practicable and Economical Route for a Railroad from the Mississippi River to the Pacific Ocean.* 12 vols. Washington, 1855–1860.

Taft, Robert. *Artists and Illustrators of the Old West 1850–1900.* Charles Scribner's Sons, New York, 1953.

Wagner, Henry R. *The Plains and the Rockies: A Bibliography of Original Narratives of Travel and Adventure 1800–1865.* Revised and extended by Charles L. Camp. San Francisco, 1937.

Wallace, Edward S. *The Great Reconnaissance.* Little, Brown and Company, Boston, 1955.

*Index*

Abajo Peak: 52
*Arctomys Ludovicianus:* 23–24
*Arroyos:* 30
Artemisia bush: 25

Bears, grizzly: 32
Beckwith, Lieutenant E. G.: *xiii, xv*
Bellows, John: 69 n.
Benton, Thomas Hart: *xvi*
Bent's Fort: 25–26
Big Timber of Arkansas: 24–25
Blodget, Lorin: 10 n.
Book Mountain: *see* Little Mountain
Buffalo: hunt described, 20–21; becoming extinct, 21–22

Call, Anson: 71 n.
*Cañons:* 30
Carboniferous System: 26
Cedar Mountains: 64
Cedar River Valley: 66
Cochetopa Pass: *see* Coochetopa Pass
Comanches: 18–19
Congress of the United States: *xvi*
Coochetopa Pass: 41, 43, 44
Council Grove: 13

107

THE AMERICAN EXPLORATION AND TRAVEL SERIES
of which *Journey Through the Rocky Mountains and the Humboldt Mountains to the Pacific Ocean* is Number 27, was started in 1939 by the University of Oklahoma Press. It follows rather logically the Press's program of regional exploration. Behind the story of the gradual and inevitable recession of the American frontier lie the accounts of explorers, traders, and travelers, which individually and in the aggregate present one of the most romantic and fascinating chapters in the development of the American domain. The following list is complete as of the date of publication of this volume.

1. Captain Randolph B. Marcy and Captain George B. McClellan. *Adventure on Red River:* Report on the Exploration of the Headwaters of the Red River. Edited by Grant Foreman.

2. Grant Foreman. *Marcy and the Gold Seekers:* The Journal of Captain R. B. Marcy, with an account of the Gold Rush over the Southern Route. Out of print.

3. Pierre-Antoine Tabeau. *Tabeau's Narrative of Loisel's Expedition to the Upper Missouri.* Edited by Annie Heloise Abel. Translated from the French by Rose Abel Wright. Out of print.

4. Victor Tixier. *Tixier's Travels on the Osage Prairies.* Edited by John Francis McDermott. Translated from the French by Albert J. Salvan.

5. Teodoro de Croix. *Teodoro de Croix and the Northern Frontier of New Spain, 1776–1783.* Translated from the Spanish and edited by Alfred Barnaby Thomas.

6. A. W. Whipple. *A Pathfinder in the Southwest:* The Itinerary of Lieutenant A. W. Whipple During His Exploration for a Railway Route from Fort Smith to

Los Angeles in the Years 1853 & 1854. Edited and annotated by Grant Foreman. Out of print.

7. Josiah Gregg. *Diary & Letters*. Two volumes. Edited by Maurice Garland Fulton. Introductions by Paul Horgan.

8. Washington Irving. *The Western Journals of Washington Irving*. Edited and annotated by John Francis McDermott. Out of print.

9. Edward Dumbauld. *Thomas Jefferson, American Tourist:* Being an Account of His Journeys in the United States of America, England, France, Italy, the Low Countries, and Germany.

10. Victor Wolfgang von Hagen. *Maya Explorer:* John Lloyd Stephens and the Lost Cities of Central America and Yucatán.

11. E. Merton Coulter. *Travels in the Confederate States:* A Bibliography. Out of print.

12. W. Eugene Hollon. *The Lost Pathfinder:* Zebulon Montgomery Pike.

13. George Frederick Ruxton. *Ruxton of the Rockies*. Collected by Clyde and Mae Reed Porter. Edited by LeRoy R. Hafen.

14. George Frederick Ruxton. *Life in the Far West*. Edited by LeRoy R. Hafen. Foreword by Mae Reed Porter.

15. Edward Harris. *Up the Missouri with Audubon: The Journal of Edward Harris*. Edited by John Francis McDermott.

16. Robert Stuart. *On the Oregon Trail:* Robert Stuart's Journey of Discovery (1812–1831). Edited by Kenneth A. Spaulding.

17. Josiah Gregg. *Commerce of the Prairies*. Edited by Max L. Moorhead.

18. John Treat Irving, Jr. *Indian Sketches*. Taken During

an Expedition to the Pawnee Tribes (1833). Edited and annotated by John Francis McDermott.

19. Thomas D. Clark (ed.). *Travels in the Old South, 1527–1860:* A Bibliography. Three volumes. Volumes One and Two issued as a set (1956); Volume Three (1959).

20. Alexander Ross. *The Fur Hunters of the Far West.* Edited by Kenneth A. Spaulding.

21. William Bollaert. *William Bollaert's Texas.* Edited by W. Eugene Hollon and Ruth Lapham Butler.

22. Daniel Ellis Conner. *Joseph Reddeford Walker and the Arizona Adventure.* Edited by Donald J. Berthrong and Odessa Davenport.

23. Matthew C. Field. *Prairie and Mountain Sketches.* Collected by Clyde and Mae Reed Porter. Edited by Kate L. Gregg and John Francis McDermott.

24. Ross Cox. *The Columbia River:* Scenes and Adventures During a Residence of Six Years on the Western Side of the Rocky Mountains Among Various Tribes of Indians Hitherto Unknown, Together with a Journey Across the American Continent. Edited by Edgar I. and Jane R. Stewart.

25. Noel M. Loomis. *The Texan–Santa Fé Pioneers.*

26. Charles Preuss. *Exploring With Frémont:* The Private Diaries of Charles Preuss, Cartographer for John C. Frémont on His First, Second, and Fourth Expeditions to the Far West. Translated and edited by Erwin G. and Elisabeth K. Gudde.

27. Jacob H. Schiel. *Journey Through the Rocky Mountains and the Humboldt Mountains to the Pacific Ocean.* Translated from the German and edited by Thomas N. Bonner.